# GUNKS TRAILS

## A Ranger's Guide to
## the Shawangunk Mountains

**Edward G. Henry**

BLACK·DOME

Published by
Black Dome Press Corp.
1011 Route 296
Hensonville, New York 12439
www.blackdomepress.com
Tel: (518) 734-6357

Copyright © 2003 Edward G. Henry

All rights reserved. No part of this publication may be reproduced in any form,
stored in a retrieval system, or transmitted in any form by any means, electronic,
mechanical, photocopying, recording or otherwise, except by a newspaper or
other reviewer who wishes to quote brief passages in connection with a review,
without prior written permission from the publisher.

ISBN: 1-883789-38-9

 Library of Congress Cataloging-in-Publication Data

Henry, Edward G.
  Gunks trails : a ranger's guide to the Shawangunk Mountains / by
Edward G. Henry ; [photographs by Edward G. Henry].
     p. cm.
  ISBN 1-883789-38-9 (pbk.)
  1. Hiking--New York (State)--Shawangunk Mountains--Guidebooks. 2.
Trails--New York (State)--Shawangunk Mountains--Guidebooks. 3.
Shawangunk Mountains (N.Y.)--Guidebooks.  I. Title.

  GV199.42.N652S534 2003
  796.52'09747'3--dc22

                         2003052380

The maps in this book were created using TOPO! Interactive Maps from National
Geographic Maps. To learn more about digital map products from National
Geographic Maps, please visit www.nationalgeographic.com/topo

Photographs by Edward G. Henry

Cover Design by Carol Clement, Artemisia, Inc.

Printed in the USA

5  4  3  2  1

*To my parents:*
*Thanks for all your love and support.*

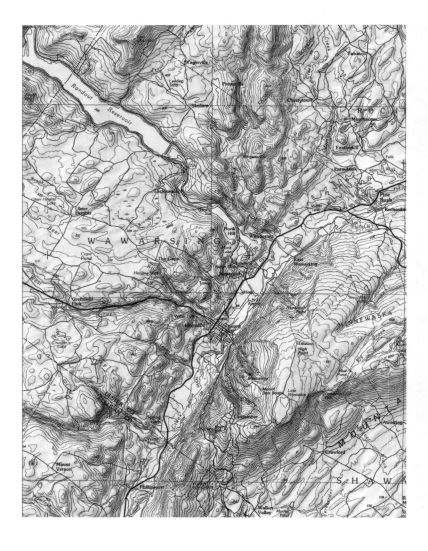

Maps created from TOPO!© National Geographic (www.nationalgeographic.com/topo)

The Shawangunks are located in southeastern New York approximately
80 miles north of New York City and 70 miles south of Albany.

# CAUTION

*Outdoor recreational activities are by their very nature potentially hazardous and contain risk. All participants in such activities must assume the responsibility for their own actions and safety. No book can replace good judgment. The outdoors is forever changing. The author and the publisher cannot be held responsible for inaccuracies, errors or omissions, or for changes in the details of this publication, or for the consequences of any reliance on the information contained herein, or for the safety of people in the outdoors.*

# HIKING RULES AND GUIDELINES

1. Dress appropriately—cotton clothing and sneakers are the number one cause of illness and injury leading to emergency evacuation. Wear proper sun protection—hat, sunglasses, sunscreen—appropriate to the season. Wear and use appropriate snow gear when the trails are snow-covered.
2. Be prepared: have a map, a compass, a first aid kit, whistle, flashlight, matches, small tarp, extra high-energy food, and water (at least 24 ounces per person). Do not drink untreated water from streams.
3. Do not use or create shortcuts. These can be dangerous and encourage erosion.
4. Respect private property rights. Do not trespass. Get permission before entering private land.
5. Camping and campfires are not allowed in the Shawangunks.

*And remember: if you carry it in, carry it out!*

# CONTENTS

The Trapps from the Old Minnewaska Carriageway

# FOREWORD

The Shawangunk Mountains are one of New York's greatest natural resources. The "Gunks," as they are popularly called, are recognized for their national and regional importance and are a destination for an estimated 500,000 visitors each year who come to enjoy bicycling, hiking, climbing, nature study and other outdoor activities. New York State recognized the significance and uniqueness of the Shawangunk Ridge in its *2002 NYS Open Space Conservation Plan*. The plan mentions the exemplary natural communities found along the Ridge and the more than twenty-five known rare plant and animal species found in the Shawangunk Mountains. The *Open Space Conservation Plan* further states:

> "Taken together these elements of biodiversity make the Shawangunks one of the highest priority areas for biodiversity conservation in the northeastern United States. ... The unfragmented forest and barrens and the fractured bedrock aquifer of the Shawangunks assure high quality ground and surface water flow ..." to the Rondout and Wallkill Valleys.

The Nature Conservancy, our nation's largest nonprofit conservation organization, has rightly deemed the Ridge one of the "Last Great Places." The Ridge boasts a rich history of conservation and public enjoyment spanning from the conservation tradition begun in the late 1800s by the Smiley family to the creation of Minnewaska State Park Preserve and Sam's Point Preserve. It is fair to say that the Ridge is a large part of what defines our region and draws people to live in this area.

Ed Henry's vivid description of the geology, geography and ecology of the Ridge perfectly defines the unique natural and cultural character of the Gunks. By reading his account of the Ridge, one can easily understand why renowned naturalists like John Burroughs would travel to the Ridge to "find themselves." He brings the ecosystems of the Shawangunk Mountains to life in his pages and reminds all of us why we should appreciate the beauty of our natural environment.

Maurice D. Hinchey
U.S. Congressman
Ulster County, New York

# PREFACE

Views and rocks are what the Shawangunks (pronounced shon-gums) promise—and they deliver. Capped by a layer of hard, white conglomerate, the Shawangunks maintain their valiant fight against the elements. A drive though the heart of the range, either along Routes 44/55 from Highland to Kerhonkson or along Ulster County Route 6 from New Paltz to High Falls, provides access to this rugged land. From rocky outposts the mountains share a wealth of views in all directions, ranging from the sea-level Hudson River to the 4,180-foot peak of the Catskills' Slide Mountain. The resistant beds of Shawangunk rocks make this ridge a rock-climbing Mecca, yet there is much more to these mountains. In addition to vistas and cliffs, there are visits to roaring waterfalls, sublime lakes and lush forests.

The Shawangunks run from Kingston to Port Jervis, but I have limited this book's scope to the area between NY Routes 213 at High Falls and 52 east of Ellenville. It is within these bounds that the knife-edge ridge widens and lifts to attain its greatest features. North of this area, the ridge decays as the white conglomerate collapses into crumbling piles among rolling hills. To the south the ridgeline is easily traversed by roads and dotted with homes, making its highlights accessible by car, yet losing the wild character preserved and reborn between Sam's Point and the Northeast Crags.

The hikes and walks present the best of the Shawangunks and their diversity. Almost all of the destinations have multiple access routes. Selected trails present the most interesting or more direct way to reach these landmarks. In many cases loop hikes provide additional scenery and underscore the ridge's incredible range of habitats. A few of the hikes traverse areas outside of the Shawangunks. Their addition enhances the overall experience of exploring the mountains as they provide a wide overview of the ridgeline.

The book is split into four sections, the first three lying along the mountains' northeast to southwest axis. Hikes along the northernmost section run from Bonticou Crag and the Northeast Crags to the famed ground around the Mohonk Mountain House and the world-famous Trapps. The central section explores the area mostly covered by Minnewaska State Park Preserve. Sam's Point Dwarf Pine Ridge Preserve overlies most of the book's southern section. The off-the-ridge section includes hikes off the eastern and western sides of the ridge, providing additional scenic and ecological means to appreciate the Shawangunks and their place in the complex geology, geography and ecology of southeastern New York State.

# ACKNOWLEDGMENTS

My decision to write about the Shawangunks was an easy one. After completing my books on the Catskills, I sat down with Debbie Allen at Black Dome Press and we asked the question, "What next?" The Shawangunks were already well known to me, and as a constant companion within the Catskills' viewshed, they seemed an obvious choice. "The Gunks!" we said in unison. After that, it was a labor of love. Hiking trails to places such as Bonticou Crag, Beacon Hill and Sam's Point, and a chance to photograph the Gunks' scenery was labor to savor.

I want to thank the many people that helped me through the process of writing this book. Many people assisted in different ways. From those who hiked the trails with me, such as Shawn Keizer, John Butnor, Nhan Bui, and Kim Keizer, to those who helped shape the book's ideas and structure, including my mother, Kim Halpin, Ly Bui and John Butnor, I owe a great deal of thanks.

In addition I want to thank the people that have supported me as I worked to balance this book into all of life's other activities. Without the friendship and love of my parents, my sister and her family, the Bui family, the Keizers, Kathy and Eric Whittemore, Jeff Underwood, Rick Jorgensen, Mike Olexa and Debbie Willis, I could not imagine finishing a book project such as this.

Hiking, photography and writing are only half the story when it comes to putting out a book. Without the kindness, friendship and professionalism of Black Dome Press—Debbie Allen and Steve Hoare specifically—there would be no *Gunks Trails*, nor any of my other books for that matter. Carol Clement continues to work her magic on the graphics and layout. Proofreaders Matina Billias and Ed Volmar did their usual outstanding job, and special thanks go to licensed hiking guide Patricia Murphy of High Land Flings for lending her intimate knowledge of the Shawangunks to her critique of the manuscript. I also want to thank the staff of the Mohonk Mountain House for their help with background materials on their site, and tips about access.

I first met Congressman Maurice Hinchey when I was a junior at Onteora High School and he was debating his challenger in our school auditorium. I have followed his career of public service ever since. His dedication to the Shawangunks and New York State demonstrates his strong commitment to the environment and the people that work so hard for conservation. I am grateful for his contribution to this book.

Blocks of Shawangunk conglomerate

# Welcome to the Shawangunks

The warm sun shines on an exposed white ledge. Strong winds provide a refreshing coolness to the air, but it is not quite enough to banish the heat. A spectacular view unfolds from the rock platform, the land falling away first as a cliff and then as a series of rocky slopes before easing in a wide, rounded valley. On the valley's far side, the land lifts again as a higher set of green-clad mountains. Yellow-green pitch pine needles border the open rock ledge, and a thick carpet of blueberries hems the scene. The sweet, plump berries provide a tasty treat. Overhead a raven circles lazily, its distinct "kruk, kruk" filling the air. Except for during or right after a storm, water is a stranger here.

Mountains are not what typically come to mind when most people think of southeastern New York. Sandwiched between the older, history-filled Hudson Highlands and the higher, geologically younger Catskills, the Shawangunks blend into the hills and valley of southeastern New York. Although best known for its rock-climbing culture, the Shawangunks are a natural haven for hikers, birders, bikers and outdoor enthusiasts. Breathtaking views and other natural treasures are commonplace when exploring the Shawangunks. From the Taconics to the east, to the Catskills to the west, the Shawangunks' bold, bleached cliffs are part of the many vistas enriching the Empire State.

Situated close to the great cities of the Northeast, it is surprising that more visitors do not come to this retreat. To most people the Shawangunks, often referred to as the Gunks, are merely a set of low hills and a few white cliffs that rise along the western side of the New York State Thruway between Newburgh and Kingston. Travelers leaving the interstate and heading into the Gunks will experience one of the most impressive landscapes in the northeastern United States.

The name Shawangunk is probably of Indian origin, but there may be a Dutch influence as well. The British used the name Chawongong to describe the area. The Delaware Indians referred to this area as

Schawaneu, meaning "south." Other tribes used the name Schunemunk, meaning "white rocks." Some historians think the name evolved from the stream running along the ridgeline's southeastern slope.

## GEOGRAPHY

From almost any approach, bold white cliffs create a rugged first impression of the Shawangunks. Sharp and foreboding, its coarse ridgeline lifts more than 1,700 feet from the surrounding valleys, topping off at 2,289 feet above sea level. The range begins just south of Kingston, lifting from the Hudson Valley as a series of steep hills. The 700-foot Snake Hill is the first of many irregular crests. A series of rocky knolls and lakes stretches to the southwest—the main axis of the entire range. Extensive caves pocket the area, many commercialized for document storage for governments and major corporations. Entrances to these underground caverns can be found throughout the area. Overall, this region, tamed by development, offers little in the way of exploration.

The area explored by this book begins south of the Rondout Creek where it carves its way through the ridge at High Falls. Although a few outcrops of the white Shawangunk conglomerate emerge to form rocky fingers and roughen the landscape, the area is still dominated by softer shales. With the taming of High Falls for hydroelectric power, and its proximity to towns and roads, the roaring plunge is more a highlight of man's economy than nature's ecology. The Gunks' main mass arises south of the Rondout Creek and is hemmed on its eastern flank by the Wallkill Valley. Along the southeastern part of the mountains, the Shawangunk Kill, a tributary of the Wallkill River, drains the mountain slopes. The Rondout Creek gathers the water from the western half of the range.

Between the area where NY 213 and NY 52 cross through the Gunks lies the area offering the most to the explorer. The ridgeline continues to the southwest, but it is more limited in width and elevation.

Sky Top from the Wallkill Valley

Roads crisscross the ridge, and the land loses any sense of wilderness. At the New Jersey state line the Shawangunks relinquish their name, handing it off to the Kittatinny Mountains, yet the ridge's common geology remains intact. In one form or another this ridge, which separates the Appalachian Mountains from the Allegheny Plateau, continues into Alabama. Other significant features along this ridge include the Delaware Water Gap, Seneca Rocks in West Virginia, and Lookout Mountain in Tennessee.

In between state highways 213 and 52, an area entirely within Ulster County, the Shawangunks reach their widest and tallest points. Like a snake that ate a huge meal, the Gunks have a wide bulge that matures the ridgeline into a small mountain range. It is this area, which extends to six miles at its center, that holds the range's most impressive destinations. A series of streams cuts the area into parallel ridges and valleys as the range thickens. When heading along the eastern or western edge of the mountains, it is hard to detect the bulge, but the east-west distance between New Paltz and Kerhonkson (18 miles) versus that of Stone Ridge and High Point (7 miles) illustrates this difference.

Routes 44/55 wind through the high area and provide many access points.

US Route 209 parallels the Shawangunks' western face. A scenic drive, this road is one of the oldest highways in America and at one time was the major link between the Hudson and Delaware valleys. This route provides access to all the major roads crossing the Gunks. Although not as steep as the Gunks' eastern side, the western slopes are still impressive, with open rock faces and a few cliffs adding character to the building elevations. At Stone Ridge, US 209 intersects NY 213. County Route 6 then heads south and east from High Falls, passing the Mohonk Mountain House before reaching New Paltz. In Kerhonkson, Routes 209 and 44/55 merge. In Ellenville, Route 52 heads southeast to cross the Gunks just south of Sam's Point. On the eastern side of the range, County Route 7 twists and turns its way along the mountains, providing a series of glimpses of the range.

Within the Gunks, a well-developed set of carriageways and foot trails crisscross the mountains. Mainly a product of the two great hotels serving the area in the late 1800s, the system has decayed some, with more of the trails near the still-operating Mohonk Mountain House remaining in good repair. Since the Shawangunks lie on a northeast-southwest axis, most of the trails following the ridgeline also use this axis; the trails cutting across the parallel valleys tend to have a northwest-southeast course. With the Hudson Valley running in a north-south line, and the front edge of the neighboring Catskills running more or less parallel with the Gunks' western margin, views and distances seem to change disproportionately with movement.

Due to their proximity, the Catskills and Shawangunks are often grouped together as one set of mountains, but each has a distinct geologic history, an independent story of formation and distinct rock structures. The two are certainly geologic cousins, but each is a range of its own. The Rondout and Esopus valleys separating the two ranges formed because of the rock structures upholding each set of mountains.

## CLIMATE

The Shawangunks lie at the boundary between the milder climate of the Hudson Valley and the cooler conditions prevalent to the north and west. The mountains' proximity to the Hudson Valley allows for the warm, moist air that moderates New York City's climate to reach the Shawangunks; however, the cold air covering the Catskills and points north and west can also reach the Gunks. In the winter this combination often results in ice accumulation. Conditions in the Shawangunks are a bit cooler and wetter than those in the Wallkill Valley to the east, but are very similar to those in the Rondout Valley to the west.

Overall the Shawangunks receive about forty-eight inches of annual precipitation, but only about half of it falls during the growing season. Between five and eight days each month have precipitation of more than .1 inches, with March through May being the most likely to include rain or snow. Thunderstorms affect the Gunks about thirty-one

Beech leaves in winter

days each year. The most rainfall recorded in a day was 6.35 inches, which fell in August of 1955. Included among the total precipitation is an average of sixty-eight inches of snow. Snow of one inch or more covers the ground an average of fifty days per year. Record snowfall for one season is 115 inches, which fell in the winter of 1966-67. The least amount of snowfall for a season was sixteen inches, recorded in 1912-13.

When averaged over the year, the temperature in the Gunks is 48F degrees, about 5F degrees lower than West Point and 8F degrees higher than the neighboring Catskills' higher elevations. July's average high temperature is 79F degrees. In January, the coldest month, the average high hovers just below the freezing mark, while nightly low temperatures average 17F degrees. The lowest temperature recorded in the Gunks was -19F degrees in January of 1957; the highest temperature recorded was 97F degrees in July of 1966.

The Shawangunks are cooler and receive a little more precipitation than the Hudson and Wallkill valleys to the east. Within the Shawangunks, the northern and western slopes receive about three more inches of annual precipitation than the southern and eastern faces. In contrast with the Gunks, the Catskills, which rise a few miles to the west, are much cooler and receive much more moisture. This difference is quite apparent on many December and March days when the Gunks are free of snow, but the Catskills glow in their winter whites.

## GEOLOGY
### The Rocks

The Gunks are composed of two main types of rock. One of them, Shawangunk conglomerate, is what brings this elongated ridge its world-wide notoriety in climbing circles and upholds the range's magnificent cliffs. The white or buff-colored rock is among the hardest in the Appalachian Mountains. It erodes slowly, even in comparison to the harder rocks upholding the Catskills and Adirondacks. Massively

Gertrude's Nose

bedded, it is often hard to distinguish one layer from another. The rock is a natural concrete made of cemented sand grains deposited at the edge of an ancient inland sea between 445 and 420 million years ago. The conglomerate, usually 200–300 feet thick, is composed almost exclusively of silica. Many variations of the rock occur, most derived from different river and bank deposits along ancient deltas and shorelines. Sandstones, quartzite and conglomerate are all part of this resistant bed. The slow erosion rate prevents the Gunks from accumulating thick, fertile soils. As a result, the local vegetation lacks diversity and nutrients. Without nutrient inputs from mineral rich bedrock, acidic conditions dominate the streams and forests.

Shawangunk conglomerate is the ancient remains of a nearly extinct mountain chain, the Taconics. The Taconic Mountains formed and grew between 500 and 445 million years ago. The Iapetus Ocean, similar to the North Atlantic in size, collapsed as it subducted beneath what is now Europe and North America. As this ancient seabed dropped below the lighter continental masses, friction and other forces created a huge trench and an arc of volcanic islands. Like the Cascade ranges of the North American west coast, a set of mountains, some volcanic, grew along what is now North America's east coast.

The mountain building was over by the end of the Silurian Period. As the Taconic Mountains eroded, they were carried away by streams and rivers. These rivers emptied into an inland sea, dropping their sediment loads in a wide series of deltas, much like the east coast of today. Together, this collection of deltas is called the Queenston Delta and extends as far west as Ohio. Most of the delta is covered by the younger sediments of the Catskill Delta, and the rock layers forming the Gunks reside beneath the Catskills. The Shawangunks are the easternmost edge of the Queenston Delta, closest to the original Taconic Mountains.

Beneath this layer of hard conglomerate lies a much thicker layer of Martinsburg shale. Formed from mud and silt deposited about 465 million years ago, this dark-colored rock is composed of many weak layers. The rock can be broken by hand. Where exposed, the shale erodes quickly, undermining any landform it supports. Huge chunks of conglomerate collapse where the underlying shales are removed. Unlike the conglomerate, the shales degrade into relatively fertile soils and can provide large amounts of soil in a short period of time. As a result, areas where the shale is exposed tend to support more impressive forests. Martinsburg shales also contain many Silurian fossils.

The two kinds of rocks were not deposited sequentially. There is a break, an unconformity, between the layers. During this interruption some of the top layers of the shale eroded before the Silurian conglomerates began to accumulate. The older shales were also subjected to an additional set of landmass collisions. As a result the shales are twisted and bent at odd angles. In some places, such as on Guyot Hill, the once-horizontal beds of rock stand almost vertical.

Being subjected to two mountain-building events, the Shawangunks' rock beds include some features that do not derive from the region's sedimentary history. Contorted and broken rock layers interacted with molten rock, and deposits of zinc, lead, copper and silver worked their way into the local strata. Most of these deposits are in the Ellenville area, as are veins of high quality quartz crystals once used for industry. Many specimens have made their way into museum collections. Selenite gypsum crystals, which formed when a freshwater inland sea evaporated, can be found north of Kerhonkson.

## The Land

The Shawangunks are not very high as far as mountains go; the loftiest point along the ridge (at 2,289 feet) is east of Ellenville near High Point. The same elevation is reached near the communications towers bristling along Lake Maratanza's western edge. From Manhattan, the Gunks are the closest point reaching 2,000 feet, but the neighboring Catskills soar an additional 2,000 feet, dwarfing the Shawangunk ridge. Directly east of the Shawangunks runs the Wallkill River. The riverbed lies at about 300 feet for most of its journey alongside the Gunks. As a result, the Shawangunk ridge and its sharp cliffs lift almost 2,000 feet from the neighboring Wallkill Valley. To the west,

Lake Maratanza

the drop into the Rondout Valley is almost as great. Many other crests along the Gunks lift at least 1,000 feet above the nearby valleys. Among the most distinct of these landmarks are Sky Top at 1,542 feet and Millbrook Mountain at 1,820 feet.

The Shawangunks are dying. Broken and worn, this thin mountain range, little more than a sharp ridgeline for much of its length, is just about out of geologic time. Like so many events in nature, an ending can be quite spectacular, and the Shawangunks are no exception. The key to understanding the Shawangunks' geology is to experience and recognize that the sharp cliff walls, craggy peaks and saw-tooth formations are the death knell of one of nature's more impressive surfaces. While in human terms the mountains appear unchanged throughout a lifetime, the story revealed through the strata and landscape is a dynamic biography of a rock layer that is among the most erosion-resistant in the Appalachians.

Despite the Gunks' precarious hold on their mountain status, their geologic life cycle is only waning, it is not yet over. The hard Silurian conglomerate (formed as the 20,000-foot Taconic Mountains eroded) topping the Gunks erodes much slower than most other rocks. The conglomerate is only up to 500 feet thick, and lies over weak Ordovician Martinsburg shale. The shale facilitates the conglomerate's demise as it undercuts the harder rock, which then collapses under its own weight. Once the top layer of conglomerate is removed, the shales erode quickly. Guyot Hill and Snake Rocks are two examples of fast-eroding Gunks land forms composed of Martinsburg shale.

Since the conglomerate beds are so erosion-resistant, they often defy gravity and the elements, refusing to collapse or slip away like the sands that formed them hundreds of million of years ago. Protesting their demise, the conglomerate forms a tantrum of shapes and angles before fading into oblivion. Broken by jointing and, in a few places, faulting, the conglomerate separates from the parent ridges. Pinnacles, rock cities, ice caves and other curious formations are the offspring of this long, but losing, battle. Deep vertical cracks slice into the mountainside to harbor cool, dark places. Near Sam's Point, some of these sheltered places became ice caves.

Unlike the Acadian mountain building that occurred after the Taconics orogeny and was eroded into complete extinction, the Taconics' roots remain part of the northeast's landscape. Both the Taconic Hills in New York and the Green Mountains in Vermont are uplifted remnants of what were once the roots of the Taconic Mountains. Later continental collisions pushed these rocks to the west, over younger Ordovician sedimentary rocks. The two mountain-building events that have occurred since then, the Acadian and Alleghenian, have warped and uplifted the Taconics strata, making their geologic story complex as multiple sets of mountain-building forces altered them at different times and in different ways.

The Alleghenian orogeny, the most recent uplift in North America, and the least violent uplift impacting New York, tilted the entire Shawangunk range twenty-two degrees from its original horizontal deposition, with the eastern side uplifted the most. The conglomerate was warped into a series of folds by this collision, which cemented all the continents into Pangea between 290 and 245 million years ago.

The folds are the basis for the tops of the Shawangunks' ridges (anticlines) and the bottoms of their valleys (synclines). Since the rock at the top of the anticlines is stretched, it tends to erode faster. In places, the conglomerate has eroded all the way down to the weaker shales beneath. Lake Awosting's bottom is one place where this has occurred. In addition, faulting, much of it associated with the opening of the Atlantic Ocean, created weak points in the rock and helped define some of the valleys.

A distinct pattern of parallel stream valleys oriented in line with the ridge's main axis results from the anticlines and synclines, along with a few fault lines. In the Gunks' widest sections, the area centered around Lake Awosting and Lake Minnewaska, a series of six of these valleys punctuates the mountains. It is easy to pick out these features on a shaded relief map of the region.

Shawangunk conglomerate is so resistant to erosion that it can stand for millions of years against the elements and remain intact. Thus, the rock can form cliffs that seem to dare Mother Nature or peo-

Winter scene: broken hemlock

ple to conquer them. Both have answered the call, but people have less ambitious standards when it comes to conquering the Gunks. The area is a rock climbing paradise, known for the quality, quantity and variety of its climbing routes. Climbing is prohibited in the state park, but is popular on the Trapps, Near Trapps, Bayards and the face of Millbrook Mountain.

Of all the Gunks' features, the steep slopes of exposed rocks grab the eye and imagination foremost. From where they first peek above the Rondout Valley, down along the Wallkill Valley to Sam's Point, the gleaming, white cliffs stand like a fortress wall. The cliffs exceed 400 feet in many places, with sheer drops of more than 200 feet. Vertical jointing, breaks in the conglomerate related to the geologic warping of the rock layers, set the stage for cliff formation here. Past earthquake activity also helped determine where the cliffs would later form. In winter the cliffs moderate the climate. In summer the exposed rocks bake in the sunshine. Only their light color prevents the area from heating up too much.

Glaciers also have played a big role in creating the Shawangunk landscape. The Wisconsin Ice Sheet was the most recent glacial episode, covering the area from about 100,000 years ago to 10,000 years ago. The ice, up to a mile thick, easily buried the entire area. Although more resistant to erosion, even the hard Shawangunk conglomerate received a facelift from the ice. Many of the exposed white rocks were polished, scratched and marked. The direction of the scratches indicated the direction the ice was moving. In the lower areas, the ice scraped and scoured against valley walls, enlarging the small valleys and steepening their sides. In a few of these valleys, such as Huntington Ravine, Verkeerder Kill, and Stony Kill, hanging valleys, complete with waterfalls, were created.

When the ice retreated, it further altered the landscape, dropping tons of debris held in its depths. This debris, called till, filled in the valley floors and often left a veneer of loose material atop the ridges. Much of the till, especially in the higher elevations, washed away. In some places large boulders suspended in the ice were dropped unceremoniously to become glacial erratics. Some of these chaotic boulders now stand in odd formations. Indian Rock and Patterson's Pellet are glacial erratics. Occasionally, these rocks were carried long distances. Hamilton sandstones from the Catskills, and even a few metamorphic rocks from the Adirondacks, now reside in the Shawangunks.

Exploring the Shawangunks can be as much about visiting its lakes as journeying to its mountaintops. Four major lakes adorn the ridge. One smaller, isolated lake, Mud Pond, lies between Lake Awosting and Lake Maratanza. The lakes are the result of glacial scouring, combined in some cases with moraines that dammed the valleys. The much larger Finger Lakes in central New York formed the same way. Each Shawangunk sky lake sits within the cracked and broken fissures near the top of an anticline. When the glacial ice melted, it left isolated pools of water in a few places. Rainwater continues to recharge the lakes. All of them are bounded by Shawangunk conglomerate, but some have bottoms of Martinsburg shale. Due to their location and the lack of nutrients within the Gunks, the water is acidic and few aquatic species live in the lakes. A high newt population in Lake Minnewaska is a notable exception, and fish are stocked in Lake Mohonk. The lakes are known for their deep blue and green hues.

In recent times, the small streams have continued to erode into the mountains, making their valleys wider and deeper. Sand worn from the ridge tops and carried away in flash floods coats many of the valley bottoms. Thin, organic soils have developed beneath many of the forests. In places these soils mix with sand and glacial till to form more fertile substrates.

## ECOLOGY

Life in the Shawangunks is limited by a lack of soil. Compared to most environments in the eastern United States, the area is not very biologically productive or diverse. In contrast, the valleys to either side hold some of the most fertile land in the east. As a result many plants and animals in the Gunks are adapted for accumulating the resources they need, rather than competing with other species. Overall, the Gunks' ecosystems are similar to those along the Virginia Blue Ridge. Forests along streams and in valleys can be lush and diverse, while ridge top ecosystems are simple and sparse.

The Gunks have three major forest types. The most distinctive are the pitch pine forests of the ridge top and cliffs. In some places the pines seem to grow right from the rocks. These simple ecosystems have very shallow soils and are prone to wildfires. Typically they support a lot of mountain laurel and blueberries. Considered unique and noteworthy, some of the pitch pines are naturally dwarfed, especially those growing on exposed rock outcroppings. More than 2,000 acres of this globally rare community exist within the range. These rare areas are protected, and signs generally warn hikers of the sensitive habitats.

The second major forest type are the pine-oak forests. Covering most of the higher elevations not dominated by pitch pine, these forests are full of small trees. Chestnut oak, gray birch, black birch, red maple, hemlock, northern red oak, white pine and pitch pine are the dominant trees in these areas. Soils are shallow and composed mainly

Painted trillium

of organic material, but water is more readily available than in the pitch pine forest.

In the stream valleys the forests are more developed. Up to forty tree species can be found in these areas, which have deeper soils and more plentiful water. Competition between individuals becomes the issue, rather than merely obtaining essential materials from the physical environment. These areas also support more wildlife, but most of the additional species are common in the surrounding Hudson and Rondout valleys as well. Some species such as tulip poplars, known for their straight, uninterrupted trunks, white oak and rhododendron are near the northern limits of their range.

Forest composition in the Gunks has not remained constant. When the Wisconsin Ice Sheet finally retreated about 10,000 years ago, it left a barren landscape. New seeds had to root in glacier-deposited tills. Pollen studies dating back 9,000 years indicate that the Gunks were dominated by oaks, jack pine, pitch pine and a spruce-fir forest. Jack pine and fir trees no longer live in the Gunks. Gray birch appeared later. There are signs the Indians burned the area. Soil records show that burn frequency increased dramatically about 1,600 years ago. Indians burned areas to pasture, drive prey and increase agricultural activity. In the Gunks, burning would have increased the dominance and yield of blueberries.

In the 1920s, American chestnut, a major tree species and valuable timber source, was hit by the chestnut blight. The disease killed all of the mature chestnuts, but the root systems continue to produce sprouts. Research is underway to find a cure for the blight and re-establish the American chestnut. Although some natural processes seem to offer some hope for recovery, most efforts by scientists have not had much impact and the chestnut remains a minor understory species.

Since the late 1900s, gypsy moths have devastated the Gunks' oaks. Thousands of acres were impacted by this imported caterpillar that was supposed to weave a new silk industry in the United States. Instead, the gypsy moth escaped from captivity and began to spread throughout New England. Millions of oaks and other trees have already been killed. Lately, infestation levels have been lower as natural diseases and engineered bacteria have lowered gypsy moth numbers. Red maples now cover many of the sites once dominated by oaks.

The Shawangunks are home to many animal species. Many types of migratory birds use the ridgeline as a giant road map helping them find their way north or south, depending on the season. The general slope of the mountains also produces excellent thermal currents, making the area even more attractive to birds. Some of the more common large birds soaring about the range include turkey vultures and ravens. Efforts to re-establish peregrine falcons, a species returned to the northeast from the brink of extinction, also continue.

Of the Gunks' mammal population, black bears, coyotes and bobcats are the largest wild predators. Gray wolves, fishers and panthers lived in the area at one time, but were eliminated by the early 1900s. A successful reintroduction program has returned the fisher to the area. They are very common now. Porcupines reach the southern extent of their range in the Gunks, and their numbers also have increased greatly during the past few decades. Opossums are near the northern edge of their range. Deer were almost eliminated from the area, but state management programs and natural migrations repopulated the area in the mid-1900s.

### FIRE

No examination of the Shawangunks is complete without looking at the role fire plays in maintaining its natural communities. Much of the area dries out in the summer as the sun and lack of soil conspire to evaporate the area's water. Vegetation and organic matter dry out. Lightning or human-caused wildfires become easy to start. Hot winds push and fan the flames, quickly engulfing large areas of the ridge tops. After consuming much of the built up fuel, the fire burns itself out, leaving behind charred earth and nutrients for a new generation of vegetation. The open ground reduces the competition for light. Pitch pines, blueberries and mountain laurel have seeds that can withstand fires and actually sprout better after a fire. Pitch pine and chestnut oak trees can even withstand light burns and will remain alive after fire passes through an area. Other oaks, maples, birch and beech have their numbers reduced as their flame-intolerant seeds do not re-establish so easily.

Light burns enhance forest productivity and reduce fuel loads. In recent times it is a lack of fire that threatens the area's unique natural communities. Without fire the pitch pine, chestnut oak, blueberries and mountain laurel are less able to compete. Not designed to reproduce in the shade of other species, the fire-adapted plants become fewer in number. In the meantime, wood, leaves and grasses continue to accumulate on the forest floor. Like the great Yellowstone fires in 1988, the Shawangunks' stage is being set for a hot, large fire that will threaten many more people and places than the small, periodic fires the ecosystem needs to maintain itself. The last major burn in the Shawangunks was in 1963. Much of the range has remained untouched by fire for many decades. Without the use of small, supervised burns to manage the area, it is only a matter of time when a huge fire sweeps through the Gunks, its pent-up fury engulfing much of the mountaintop and some of the surrounding terrain as well.

## ECONOMY AND MODERN LAND USE

The area's economy was originally dominated by agriculture. Although few agricultural crops grow well in the mountains, the surrounding valleys support almost everything from wheat to grapes. Apples are one of the region's largest crops. Being so close to New York City, this area grew and supplied much of the city's fresh produce. Fresh apples, which would spoil very quickly, could be brought to market directly. Photos of this area in the late 1800s show that most of the land was being used for farming. As modern transportation and refrigeration systems came into being, the need for locally produced

Purple trillium

crops declined as larger farms drove local farms into bankruptcy. Only the most fertile and productive lands in the valleys remain cultivated. Much of the land reverted to forest.

Within the mountains, blueberries and huckleberries were the main agricultural product. The two species of berries are closely related and can interbreed. Blueberries are much sweeter and have smaller seeds, but there were markets for both berries. The two berries are typically grouped together and the names used interchangeably. Although blueberries were never cultivated in this area, a migrant culture developed around the seasonal harvest.

Tourism is one of the area's biggest sources of income with about 600,000 people visiting the resorts, parks and preserves annually. Tourism patterns today are much different than they were fifty years ago. The resort hotels are no longer the area's biggest draw. Rock climbing is now a huge attraction, and the Gunks' cliffs are world-renowned. The Shawangunk conglomerate is superior for providing handholds, holding equipment and creating challenging routes. In addition, the fresh air, sky lakes and remaining hotels bring many other people into the region. The Gunks' tourism industry totals about $15 million annually.

Mining for lead, zinc and copper have added to the local economy, although none of the deposits are economically viable today because of the global economy and inexpensive transportation. In the middle of the twentieth century, quartz crystals found between Ellenville and the mountains became a big business until replaced by manmade substitutes. In the early and mid-1800s, Shawangunk conglomerate was used for making high quality mill stones. In a few places along the Trapps and Bayards, remnants of broken millstones remain among the talus piles.

Moving mining and agricultural products from this area to the nation's major cities, and bringing materials from them to the area was a major challenge for merchants and farmers in the early 1800s. The Great Valley, a series of river valleys stretching from the St. Lawrence River in Canada to the Tennessee River in Alabama, runs along the Shawangunks' western edge and presented the easiest opportunity to build transportation links to the south and west from the Hudson Valley. The Old Mine Road, one of the oldest roads in the United States, and the Delaware and Hudson Canal both took advantage of this natural passageway. The D&H Canal fell victim to the railroads, another transportation medium taking advantage of the Great Valley, but the Old Mine Road has continued to exist and is now roughly traced by U.S. Route 209.

Much of the Shawangunks' wild character has been preserved through the efforts of the Smiley family. Without their stewardship of more than 17,000 acres along the ridge top, the Gunks would not have retained a fraction of the natural value they have for visitors in modern times. Through a variety of means, stewardship of the Shawangunks now falls to four main organizations. In 1963, the Mohonk Mountain House shed more than 5,300 acres of land and created a non-profit organization, the Mohonk Trust, to oversee this area.

Renamed the Mohonk Preserve, the trust has grown to include more than 6,250 acres. The hotel retains 2,200 acres around the main building including Eagle Cliff and Sky Top.

Minnewaska State Park Preserve holds more than 10,000 acres in the central Shawangunks. This is the Gunks' widest area, where the ridge fattens and the hard conglomerate reaches its most extensive east-west coverage. The area includes what were once the Minnewaska resorts and the surrounding land base, including lakes Minnewaska, Awosting and Mud Pond. The preserve was born in 1971 when the state purchased 7,000 acres from the Lake Minnewaska resort. The two hotels burned to the ground—Cliff House in 1978 and Wildmere in 1985. Marriott Hotels had shown interest in opening a conference center in the mid-1980s, but local opposition finally convinced the state to purchase and preserve the land.

The southern part of the Shawangunks is more developed and has seen more changes in ownership. The village of Ellenville employs Lake Maratanza as a backup water supply, and has looked to protect this small watershed from development. Starting in the 1960s, Ice Caves Mountain became a major tourist attraction. Various communication towers were built atop the ridge, marring the viewshed, but maintaining much of the land's natural character. By the early 1990s the property had an uncertain future. In 1994 the land was purchased by the Open Space Institute, a conservation agency, and subsequently became Sam's Point Dwarf Pine Ridge Preserve, which is managed by The Nature Conservancy. To underscore the area's scenic beauty and ecological importance, The Nature Conservancy has named the Shawangunks one of "The Earth's Last Great Places." Although the world-wide recognition is a badge of honor for this incredible natural area, it is the personal experience among huge cliffs, stalwart pitch pine and wide views that makes this area worth exploring.

# THE EASTERN RIDGE

Winter profile of Bonticou Crag

**Hike: Bonticou Crag**

**Distance:** 3.75 miles

**Parking:** Spring Hill Parking Area. Located off County Route 6 on Upper Knolls Road, 1 mile west of the entrance to the Mohonk Mountain House and 3.6 miles east of NY 213 via County Routes 6A and 6 from High Falls.

**Fees:** $5 per person, Mohonk Preserve. Yearly membership available.

**Difficulty:** Easy, with a short, difficult rock scramble.

**Elevation change:** (lowest to highest points on route): 550 feet

**GPS reference points:**

Parking Area: 41°47.710' N, 74°07.685' W

Bonticou Crag: 41°47.311' N, 74°07.076' W

**Details:**

0.00 Spring Farm Parking Area—follow dirt road or blue-marked Table Rocks Trail left (east).

0.20 Junction with red-marked Crag Trail. Head right (southeast).

0.40 Cross two carriageways (Cedar Drive and Spring Farm).

0.75 Crag Trail ends at Bonticou Carriageway. Turn left (northeast).

1.05 Junction with yellow-marked Crag Ascent Trail. Turn left (southeast).

1.20 Summit, Bonticou Crag 1,194 feet. Trail heads to left (northeast).

1.50 Crag Ascent Trail ends at blue-marked Northeast Trail. Continue straight (northeast).

2.15 Northeast Crags.

2.30 Northeast Trail ends at red-marked Clearwater Carriageway. Veer left (northwest).

2.75 Join with blue-marked Table Rocks Trail. Turn left (southwest).

3.75 Table Rocks Trail return to parking area. End of hike.

Drifting southwest from the edge of Kingston, New York, the Shawangunk ridge rises boldly from the Hudson Valley. The northern crests are all built of weak shales and sandstones. The Shawangunk conglomerate appears where Rondout Creek slices through the range. South of this junction rise the Gunks' higher, wilder places. In a few isolated spots north of the Rondout's spirited crossing, small, rocky pinnacles of conglomerate struggle to remain above the landscape, but they are only shadows of the true Shawangunks.

Once south of Rondout Creek, the Shawangunk conglomerate becomes the dominant rock and builds to the first significant crests as Northeast and Bonticou crags. In all, this strident bastion rises almost 1,000 feet above the Wallkill River near its confluence with Rondout Creek. Bonticou Crag, however, is only a small island of conglomerate-inspired elevation. South of the crag, a small tributary of the Kleine Kill cuts into the Shawangunk ridge. Utilizing the weakened line of an ancient fault, the valley isolates Bonticou Crag's bold, rocky protrusion. In all directions weak shales surround the rough and rugged conglomerate. Together, the softer terrain and near-vertical thrust of Bonticou Crag enhance the area's scenic qualities. Once, not that long ago in geologic time, Shawangunk conglomerate topped this entire area. To gain Bonticou Crag's impressive viewpoints now requires a pleasant hike through old fields and a recovering forest.

On leaving the Spring Farm parking area, the blue-marked Table Rocks Trail follows a row of trees bordering an old farm field. Grasses and open meadow cover most of the landscape since land managers arrest the natural processes that would restore the forest. By manipulating a variety of habitats, proper management creates more places for animal species to find food and shelter. In this area, where forest and field merge, cutting and mowing increases plant and animal diversity. Red foxes and white-tailed deer are two mammals well-suited to this mixed habitat. The open land also provides sweeping vistas of the surrounding area.

After heading a short distance into the field, the trail splits. The route to Bonticou Crag follows the red-marked Crag Trail. Old stone

Maps created from TOPO!© National Geographic (www.nationalgeographic.com/topo)

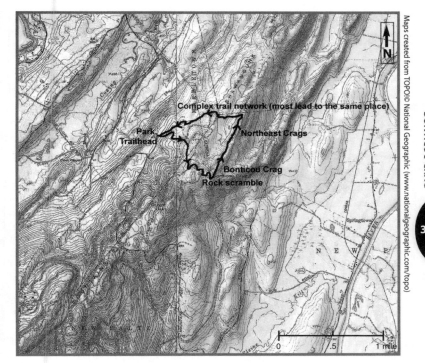

walls, once boundary markers of fields and property lines, escort the path. The walls contain a variety of rocks once embedded in these fields. Farmers cleared them as they improved the fields. After completing houses and barns and with no place to put additional rocks, farmers used the leftover material for fencing. Although most of these rocks are of local origin, glaciers also transported material from the Catskills and left it among these fields.

The open fields provide a few views west to the Catskills. Mombaccus Mountain (2,800 feet) and High Point (3,098 feet) are the most prominent. An impressive outline of the central Catskills' higher peaks lifts in the distance. Although many of the Catskills' highest peaks are part of the scene, Slide Mountain, the highest, is hidden behind High Point. To the south, the rising ridges uphold the Mohonk Mountain House and Sky Top. The elaborate Victorian hotel's grays and somber reds blend harmoniously with the landscape, despite the hotel's prominent location along the ridge. In contrast, the gothic tower defiantly protrudes into the sky—a signature Shawangunk landmark visible for miles around.

Uncrowded by neighbors, wide tree crowns, mostly oak and hickory, spread over the fields. Red cedar, a tree often associated with exhausted agricultural fields, and blue beech (also known as musclewood), easy to identify by its sinewy trunk, are also common. Among the trees lining the fields are a variety of coppiced stems, including sugar maple, red maple, white ash and northern red oak. Before this area was protected as part of the Mohonk Preserve, the land supported orchards, farm fields and pasture. First cleared for timber and to create farms, many other trees were cut for firewood. Root systems on many deciduous species continue to live and send up new sprouts after cutting. When more than one of these shoots survives, the stems typically grow away from one another to minimize competition for light. Often three or four stems will survive to produce a small ring of trunks around the original. A circle traced through the middle of the coppiced stems about a foot off the ground gives a rough approximation of the original tree's girth. Each sprout will vie for dominance, but the need for light pushes its growth away from the others. With their angled orientation, coppiced trees are unstable and subject to wind and ice damage. They rarely survive more than eighty years, and do not produce quality timber. Snapped trunks are common.

As the trail moves upslope, the open fields end and the trail moves into a young forest. Crisp leaf litter replaces soft grasses. Small trees, with scattered larger trunks of oak, shade the land. The old oaks were part of this landscape when it was still used for agriculture. The tired soils are still thick and fertile enough to support a healthy forest. Sugar maple, striped maple, shagbark hickory, beech, chestnut oak, chestnut, ironwood, witch hazel, hemlock and white pine compose the majority of the forest. Most of these species are useful as building materials or furniture, and provide local landowners with another source of income or fuel. As this stand matures, the trees will again become valuable, but this time their greatest asset will be based in ecology, not economics.

The trail gains some elevation, but overall the slopes remain gentle. The switch from sun to shade is more noticeable. Along the route, the foot trail crosses two well-maintained carriage roads, another relic of the area's past. Not all signs of past land use have disappeared. Stone fences continue uninterrupted into the forest, their outdated lines unaware of nature's revival. A few of the larger trees, mainly oaks, have the spreading forms that developed during their youth in what were then open fields. With the forest's resurgence, the spreading oaks will have to compete for light. The shade also prevents acorns from sprouting successfully. In the future, fewer oaks will be found in this forest.

Never steep, the Crag Trail ends in a small, level area, where it joins Bonticou Carriageway. The route to Bonticou Crag heads left (northeast). The wide, smooth path retains the potential to host carriages and other traffic. Small wetlands accent the junction. The glacially inspired landscape is poorly drained, especially among the headwater valleys. Annual plants such as jewelweed, stinging nettles, false Solomon's seal and skunk cabbage are common. Hemlocks also thrive near the wet areas, utilizing the extra moisture to out-compete other species and keep them from restarting by blanketing the ground in heavy shade.

As the carriageway winds around a small hill, it lifts a few feet above the headwater valley, providing a unique look into the forest canopy. The elevation boost is just enough to peer above the understory and get a good look at the taller trees' upper halves. In many ways the forest here is like a city—a few skyscrapers and lots of smaller buildings. In tree city it is competition for light that dominates the battle for real estate, and the way both the overstory and understory position themselves for the available light is reflected in the vertical profile. In the rainforests of South America and Africa, four or five separate layers are common, but in the temperate forests of eastern North America, three levels are typical—ground cover, understory and canopy—along with emergent species such as white pine.

A snowy rendition of the conglomerate talus lining Bonticou Crag's base

A distinctive trailside feature appears among some exposed rock cuts. The main geologic reason for the Shawangunks' presence is the resistant conglomerate cap rock topping the ridge. Bonticou Crag is near the northern extent of this rock, and most of the area around it, including the path to the crag, is underlain by a much weaker set of Ordovician shales. Here, the weak, crumbly shale is exposed. It erodes into soil quickly, and ferns and mosses colonize exposed outcrops. A quick touch demonstrates how quickly these rocks can erode—they easily can be broken by hand. In comparison with the conglomerate, the impact is even more pronounced. Areas without the conglomerate erode much faster, producing a landscape where Bonticou Crag is further accented. Another physical difference between the two rock layers is the shale's complex bedding—it is tilted on its side—a result of the two mountain building eras that have occurred since the shale was deposited as sediment about 465 million years ago.

Rounding another corner, the carriageway abruptly encounters Bonticou Crag's massive conglomerate ridge. The stark white conglomerate practically glows through the intervening forest, outshining the sky on all but the brightest of days. In comparison with surrounding forest, almost nothing grows on the sharp bounders and outcrops. The bulky, angular rocks jut into the sky. Shawangunk conglomerate is among the most stalwart material North America has to combat nature's unrelenting forces of erosion. Casualties from the never-ending battle lie in broken piles against the main ridge. Soils over the conglomerate become thinner and less fertile. Along the carriageway and its shale base, white pine, striped maple and paper birch are the most prominent tree species. Atop the ridgeline, pitch pines provide a buzz-cut that enhances the crag's ruggedness. The hundred-foot climb on the chaotic geology appears challenging and imposing.

The trail follows the edge of the shale and stays under forest cover. Pileated woodpeckers dart and drill into the trees. Among the area's more conspicuous birds, these woodpeckers are best known by many as the model for Woody Woodpecker. They thrive in mixed conifer-deciduous forests. Flying and bouncing from tree to tree, the flash of red often reveals their location. Although shy, the sound of their activity reverberates through the forest, especially when they drum on trees to mark their territory.

The seventeen-inch, red-crested birds have black bodies with a white stripe on their necks. Searching for insects among tree bark, they drill into their favorite trees and pull away sections of bark. They also spend a lot of time on the ground searching for food among dead and rotting logs. Carpenter ants and beetle larvae are their favorite foods. On occasion they will eat fruits and nuts. If there is no dead wood on the ground, pileated woodpeckers will move to better habitat. Like many of the Gunks' forests, this bird benefits from the fires that keep the understory open and promote the growth (and death) of pines.

Pairs generally bond for many years. Males and females share responsibility for roosting eggs, protecting territory and providing food for their young. Pileated woodpeckers only nest in pine trees, and in this region white pine are preferred. A few use pitch pine. The females make a cavity in their selected nesting trees and then peck holes around the opening to keep a flow of sticky sap around the nest, discouraging predators from entering. Sometimes they nest in dead trees. The birds lay from two to four eggs each year.

Once around the small hill, the Bonticou Carriageway meets the western terminus of the short, steep Crag Ascent Trail. A sign notes the danger inherent in climbing the rugged terrain. The thin yellow-marked trail dives into a small divide before emerging from the forest at the jagged rock wall. On a sunny day, the reflection off the white rock is blinding. The trail immediately attacks the terrain, ascending a rough and rocky face. The trail is lightly worn—another testament to the rock's strength. Rounded quartz pebbles are embedded in the natural concrete. Most of these rounded stones washed down during ancient floods. Winding, twisting and bending, the trail threads its way up the cliff. A few lichens and the occasional pitch pine or mountain laurel are the only signs of trailside life, and even the vegetation is sparse. As the trail climbs, a few views begin to open to the northeast and southwest, but improved versions await on the crag.

The trail begins to ease before reaching ridge top. Pockets of sandy soil harbor mountain laurel, huckleberries and blueberries. Pitch pine and paper birch are the dominant trees. Few of the trees rise more than fifteen feet high, and most are windblown and ragged. The warmer colors of the neighboring shales reveal how closely rock type can relate to forest development. Rusty pine needles fill many of the cracks and spaces between the rocks, adding to the local harsh color scheme. Once the trail levels off, it merges onto the relatively level conglomerate backbone that protrudes like an armored spine. A few steps to the southwest is Bonticou Crag's summit. Although not high at 1,194 feet, the views are impressive, enhanced by the nearly 1,000 feet of elevation gain from the neighboring Wallkill Valley. To the south, the ridgeline collapses, interrupted by an old fault and filled by an intermittent tributary of the Kleine Kill.

The opening of the land on a southeast-northwest axis, opposite the main trend of the Shawangunk range, provides the foundation for the crag's extraordinary views. To the southeast, the populated landscape presents a more pastoral scene than the forests and mountains to the northwest. New Paltz lies a bit south of east, easily identified by the university's towers. The wide Wallkill Valley fills the foreground, and bordering its eastern edge are the Plattekill Mountains, anchored by Illinois and Marlboro mountains. In the distance is the Hudson Valley, and beyond it rise the Taconics. To the southwest sits the Guyot Hill's rounded, forested summit. Although almost 100 feet higher than Bonticou Crag, Guyot Hill is topped only by weak Ordovician shales and is the Gunks' highest point not capped by conglomerate.

To the northwest the view takes in most of the eastern Catskills. The Rondout and Esopus valleys separate the two mountain ranges, with the Esopus Valley heading into the central Catskills and dividing the range into two groups of high peaks. Rising almost due west, Slide Mountain, in the southern group, rises to 4,180 feet—the Catskills' highest point. High Point, which eclipses the view of Slide from the open fields, stands engulfed by the Catskill giant. Other notable peaks include Cornell and Wittenberg mountains. In the northern group, Westkill, Hunter, and the Devil's Path are most prominent. Along the Catskills' northeastern edge, Overlook Mountain forms a distinct corner, slightly closer than the other peaks. The fire tower atop the 3,180-foot peak provides a good view back to the Shawangunks.

Perhaps as impressive as the view is something that cannot be seen. Directly beneath Bonticou Crag, about 700 feet below the surface, flows the Catskill Aqueduct, which delivers water from the northern Catskills to New York City. The entire structure is gravity-powered, using the difference in elevation between the reservoir (587 feet above sea level) and New York City (sea level) to pull water down to the city. Although it is a magnificent engineering feat of the early twentieth century, when considered in terms of where the water goes, the whole system is almost comical. After all, the Catskills' water that enters the Ashokan Reservoir would have flowed into the Hudson and right past New York City anyway! Of course, what happens to that water in terms of quality and salinity is another story altogether.

From Bonticou Crag the yellow trail heads northwest, following the rock spine to another set of views—the Northeast Crags. Although less extensive, the view is still impressive and worth the trip. After a descent, the Crag Trail ends at the blue-marked Northeast Trail. The trail follows the crags' ridgeline, passing though a forest of pitch pine, chestnut oak, paper birch, mountain laurel and blueberries—a classic fire-driven forest system. In spring a few sites harbor pink lady slippers, a member of the orchid family. As the land continues to fall, the soils have more opportunity to accumulate, and black birch and northern red oak join the forest.

The Northeast Crags open in a series of two westerly views stretching from the south—including Bonticou Crag—to the northwest and the Catskills. Lone and Rocky mountains, two of the lesser known and harder to identify Catskill summits, stand out from this perspective. Unfortunately poor air quality, mainly from sulfur, nitrogen and humidity, often limit the vista. Beneath the crag, white pine emerge from the forest canopy. The tree's flexible woods give it the ability to surge above its neighbors into the weather and survive. Risks from ice and wind are offset by the additional light the tree can gather. The strategy must work, for if it did not the white pines would not have been able to survive and reproduce.

Once beyond the crags, the trail drops quickly and sharply off the northern edge of the Shawangunk conglomerates. North of this point, Shawangunk conglomerate reappears only as broken outcrops. The Northeast Trail ends here, and the route follows the Clearwater Road west. Once off the conglomerate, a mixed forest returns to the land. The area is crisscrossed by small streams to produce a mountain wetland. Hemlocks dominate much of the forest, their deep gloom cooling the air and keeping other vegetation at bay. The wetland is home to many amphibians and insects, and while it is not a pleasant place for people, the wetlands are biologically productive and support many species of plants and animals that would not be able to survive elsewhere in this region.

After a short walk though the deciduous forest, Clearwater Road ends at the blue-marked Table Rocks trail. The trail and a farm road both return to the parking area. Heading again into open fields, the route provides limited views, and some good bird-watching opportunities. Killdeer is one notable species. The best route back to the parking area varies based on season and weather conditions.

Although nestled at the northern edge of the Gunks and the lowest of its viewpoints, Bonticou Crag is among the most impressive spots to experience the massive layers of Shawangunk conglomerate. Its northerly position also gives it some of the best views into the northern Catskills, a much higher set of mountains. The juxtaposition of field and forest, wet and dry, and hard rock and soft ground produces a mix of environments that helps make this area a place worth exploring any time of the year.

Looking across Lake Mohonk to Sky Top

**Hike: Eagle Cliff**
**Distance:** 1.9-mile loop
**Parking:** Take County Route 6 from the east or west side of the ridge. Turn into the Mohonk Mountain House entrance way. Parking areas are located near the entrance and at the hotel. A shuttle is available from the entrance parking area to the hotel.
**Fees:** $15 for car and driver plus $5 additional per individual
**Difficulty:** Easy, with a few steep, rocky spots
**Elevation Change:** (Lowest to highest points on route) 360 feet
**GPS Reference Points:**

| | |
|---|---|
| Hotel: | 41°46.097'N, 74°09.330'W |
| Eagle Ascent Path: | 41°45.696'N, 74°09.694'W |
| Copes Lookout: | 41°45.895'N, 74°09.686'W |

**Details:**

0.00 Start from south end of Mohonk Mountain House at beginning of Eagle Cliff Carriageway. There are also many side trails paralleling the carriageway.

0.50 Reach summit of Eagle Cliff, elevation 1,434 feet. Turn left on red-marked Eagle Ascent Path.

0.60 End of Eagle Ascent Path; turn right (west) on Short Woodland Drive.

0.65 Short Woodland Drive ends at Humpty Dumpty Carriageway. Turn right (north) on Humpty Dumpty Carriageway.

0.75 Turn left on the blue-marked spur trail, which runs into the Giant's Path.

1.05 Giant's Path heads left at the red-marked Arching Rocks Path. Continue straight. For the side trip to Giant's Workshop, turn left and follow the Giant's Path, then return to the Arching Rocks Path.

1.40 Arching Rocks Path ends at the blue-marked Cathedral Path. Turn right (uphill).

1.50 Cathedral Path ends at Copes Lookout. Turn left on Laurel Ledge Carriageway. After only a few steps, the Copes Lookout Path forks to the right.

1.80 Copes Lookout Path ends on Eagle Cliff Carriageway. Turn left.

1.90 Return to Mohonk Mountain House. End of hike.

The Mohonk Mountain House is a bastion of nineteenth-century culture and refinement embedded in a sea of twentieth-century recycled wilderness. To walk the hotel grounds is an experience outside the definitions of most modern-day hikes. It is easy to imagine the steady clop-clop-clop of horse-drawn buggies and whispers of long-past conversations among proper ladies and gentlemen on the carriageways. Gazebos and benches pepper the landscape, providing seating and shade as they overlook some of the Gunks' best scenery.

In 1963 amid rising taxes and operating costs, the Smiley family, owners and operators of the Mohonk Mountain House, divided their 7,500 acres into two parts. The first included the hotel and a core of surrounding land, about 2,200 acres. The remaining 5,300 acres were set aside as the Mohonk Preserve.

Within the lands retained by the hotel are two of the Shawangunks' most recognizable points: Sky Top and Eagle Cliff. These two promontories surround Lake Mohonk and frame the hotel. The points remain favored destinations for hotel guests and visitors. Of the two, Eagle Cliff is the harder to access when not beginning from the hotel's grounds. It is one of the Gunks' most scenic perches, with spectacular views of the Shawangunks and the neighboring Catskills.

While some of the original defining experiences of visiting the hotel have faded and blurred with the years, hiking on the hotel grounds is an adventure unlike any other in the United States. A vast network of manicured, crisscrossing trails and carriageways overlie the land like a complex spider web. The gazebos are well maintained and the trails are smooth. Hiking around the hotel is not difficult or challenging. The paths were made to be gentle retreats, not catalysts for physical exertion. With so many places to stop and the trails'

Maps created from TOPO!© National Geographic (www.nationalgeographic.com/topo)

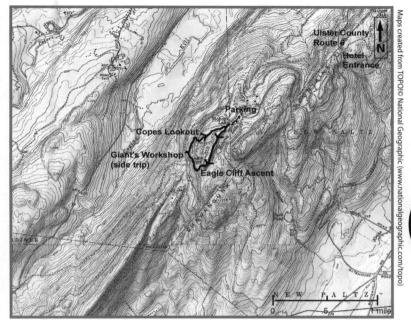

**45**

winding layout, there is little chance to develop a rhythm or a sweat. Only in a few places does the terrain become more challenging—a strong contrast to the gentle trails and carriageways.

The Mohonk experience begins as the hotel's entrance road sprouts off Ulster County Route 6. The drive to the hotel parking areas is 2.2 miles on a winding, leisurely road. Walking and hiking trails radiate from the pavement to head for all corners of the hotel property and surrounding preserve. Although covered in forest, the landscape shows constant signs of man's attention and nature's forces. Fences, blowdowns and erosional features escort the roadway. The forest is mainly pine and oak, with slope and orientation playing a big role in determining which trees dominate an area—pines on the south and west-facing slopes; oak, red maple and birch on the north and east-facing ones.

A shuttle is available in season to take day visitors from the entrance gate to the hotel. When driving to the hotel, look for parking areas to the right (downhill) of the hotel. Signs help guide drivers to the parking areas. The hotel's manicured grounds are legendary, yet their appearance in contrast with the woods still comes as a surprise. The hotel is open only to guests and pass holders, so to reach the Eagle Point Carriageway, non-registered hikers must skirt the hotel grounds. To begin the hike from within the hotel, the best place to start is from the porch facing Lake Mohonk.

The hotel grounds are filled with well-tended gardens and landscapes. Stone walls and dark green and brown painted wood rise from the lake in manmade mimicry of the nearby mountains and forests. The hotel's fingers reach into the adjoining sky, forest and water. To see the hotel and its grounds is to look through time as well as space. Eagle Cliff stretches south of the Mountain House like an elongated and slightly flattened version of Sky Top. Lake Mohonk lies along the cliff's eastern edge, the deep blue water penned by stark white cliffs.

The hike begins by following the Eagle Cliff Carriageway west, an easy, wandering climb. Since this carriageway makes almost a complete loop, it is important to start on the leg nearest the hotel. A series of well-worn, informal side trails parallels the carriageway as it climbs. The first of these meanders onto Pine Bluff and like most of the side trails provides outstanding views of the lake, the hotel and Sky Top.

The views change with each gazebo and lookout. To the northwest are a few glimpses of the Catskills, their bulk staring back at the older, lower Shawangunks. Toward the lake, a few steep and slender trails work their way down the cliff to the Undercliff Path and the water's edge. At the cliff edge, where soils are shallow and exposed bedrock is the rule, a few pitch pine and oak claim the best sites. Slightly away from the cliff edge, hemlocks become the dominant tree. Slow-growing and moisture-loving, hemlock trees benefit from the lake-influenced humidity. Their cool shade is a welcome relief from the strong summer sun. In winter their dense foliage reduces snowpack and ice formation.

Spring in the Gunks can be a harsh time. Ice is a frequent winter

A view north from Eagle Cliff back toward Mohonk Mountain House

guest, and as it melts it joins with spring rains to start the mud season. Still, many places in the Gunks are so well drained and have such shallow soils that the water evacuates quickly, leaving the sun to dry out and heat up the land. Although the diversity of plant life in the Gunks is similar to that of the surrounding areas, much of the land is inhospitable—either too dry, too exposed, or without good enough soils to support many of the species found in the neighboring valleys and the Catskills. Spring wildflowers are noticeably absent in many places, including Eagle Cliff. The crimson splashes of red maple flowers are one of the few exceptions. Red maples can tolerate a variety of sites, including dry areas with shallow soils. Their bold color among Eagle Cliff's drab spring shades is a welcome accent. The pink blossoms of mountain laurel mark spring's latter half.

In many aspects the views along Eagle Cliff's eastern edge are a showcase of Sky Top. Although it is hard to determine which spot along the carriageway is best, the visual feast in enjoying each vantage point makes the journey a slow, yet pleasant one. In some ways the views of the stone Albert Smiley tower are more impressive than those from the tower itself! Across the lake the tower proudly rises from atop the 1,542-foot peak like a medieval fortress protecting an important mountain pass. The high cliffs soar from the lake shore, rising well above the mighty hemlock and pine trunks along the lake's eastern shore. Deep joints in Sky Top's structure create black shadows on the hard white cliffs. Among the most prevalent of these is the lemon squeeze, a difficult and unique approach to the tower. Jumbled talus litters the cliff bottom like the bones of armies defeated long past. In reality, though, the talus is the ever-mounting losses in Sky Top's fight with the eternal forces of erosion.

With so many side trails, it is easy to get confused while ascending Eagle Cliff. The route is best defined by the land. Keep the lake to the left and remain along the top of the cliff, and there is no wrong way to climb Eagle Cliff. Once atop the cliff, the side trails return to the carriageway, which becomes more direct and easier to follow.

Once the carriageway outdistances the higher form of Sky Top, the view begins to change. The Wallkill and Hudson valleys, along with the intervening Plattekill Hills, replace the southeastern view-shed. New Paltz is prominent, as is Illinois Mountain with its tall transmission towers. Farther south rise the Hudson Highlands, with Mount Beacon, Storm King and West Point protecting the Hudson's flanks.

Another far-reaching viewshed unfolds to the north. The eyes can take pleasant journeys slipping along Lake Mohonk and the parallel spines of Sky Top and Eagle Cliff. Eagle Cliff leads back to the hotel, its stone turrets announcing its permanence among the landscape. Beyond the hotel the view opens over the Esopus Valley and the Catskills' eastern foothills.

Across the lake a pine-oak forest fills the valley. The oaks, along with a few maple and birch, create a level, smooth canopy. This united front protects the forest from winter ice storms by reducing the winds slicing into the forest. Situated in a prime spot where Atlantic moisture clashes with Canadian cold, the Gunks receive a lot of ice. Ice accumulations of an inch or more can coat the entire mountaintop. To the north and west there is more snow, and to the east and south there is less frozen precipitation.

A hole in the forest canopy is like an open wound. As ice accumulates on branches and strong winds buffet the heavily laden limbs, they break. Entire trees can blow down this way, and the forest opening makes future damage more likely. During the next growing season, neighboring trees will act quickly to fill the sunny gaps. New saplings, especially birch and cherry, arise from the understory. Yet, until a smooth canopy re-forms, the potential for new storm damage remains high. In places where a uniform canopy cannot develop, the forest remains dominated by pitch pine and white pine, species that can take advantage of the harsher conditions.

White pine has a different strategy for survival. Rather than share protection with neighboring species, white pines grow above the canopy as emergent trees. Although more exposed, white pines also receive more direct sunlight, allowing them to grow and repair damage faster than most other species. In addition the wood is light and flexible, giving white pine the ability to withstand the deadly combination of wind and ice. A look around the forests surrounding Lake Mohonk shows this to be a successful strategy.

As Eagle Cliff continues south, it outdistances Lake Mohonk. Without the additional humidity provided by the water, the forest loses most of its hemlock component. Chestnut oak, northern red oak, red maple, pitch pine, white pine, black birch and paper birch compose the majority of the forest. Without solid tree cover the land bakes in the sun. Luckily, breezes are common as the elevation increases. The cooler air is especially welcome in summer.

Once the side trail leaps a few last rocky outcrops, it rejoins the carriageway atop the 1,434-foot mountain. Views and vistas continue to accompany the route, keeping progress slow. Beyond the unadorned summit the land drops, and views to the south and west appear. The view down the Shawangunks' spine is one of the range's finest, demonstrating the structure of the entire ridge from an edge-on perspective. The dip of the rocks and the wavy series of synclines and anticlines are easy to see in the land's contours. Again there are many variations on the view, but all of them are dominated by the Gunks' sharp, eastern edge—the cliffs that make the range world-renowned as a rock-climbing Mecca. In the foreground lift the Trapps, then the Near Trapps, Bayards and finally, Millbrook Mountain. The wedge-shaped Coxing Kill Valley interrupts the ridge before it builds to its highest summits in Minnewaska State Park Preserve and at Sam's Point. A herd of communication towers near Lake Maratanza stud the distant ridgeline. At the cliff's base, pines and white conglomerate boulders create a stark pattern of light and dark.

Many generations have enjoyed this perch, and this vista was captured by Worthington Whittredge in his painting, *Twilight in the Shawangunks*. Whittredge, a painter of the Hudson River School, portrayed a beautiful evening scene looking to the south. Dated 1865, this piece uses subtle, almost sad tones to convey Whittredge's mourning for the loss of America's youth and idealism at the close of the Civil War. The wilderness is no longer the vigorous and imposing force many earlier Hudson River School paintings portray. Instead, the land, sky and vegetation look washed out and dull. The painting is one of the largest and most detailed of the Shawangunks. Its ability to speak through time to share the look and feel of the Shawangunks a century and a half ago adds to the timelessness of the rocks, mountains, lake and Victorian hotel.

Eagle Cliff is named for the migrating eagles and other raptors that move though the area in the spring and fall. Eagles, hawks and falcons all follow the crest of the Gunks to help guide their movements and benefit from the rising air currents. Ravens and vultures can be seen most of the year. At the cliff wall's southern tip, the Eagle Ascent Path begins its harsh, rocky route down into the forest. A few steps beyond the trail, three gazebos sit along the cliff and provide spectacular views to the south and west that include the central Catskills and the Devil's Path.

The Eagle Ascent Trail is a short, but steep route to the cliff's base. The trail is well marked with red paint. Snakes commonly bask on the chaotic, rocky ground. The path moves though a maze of white rock, even passing under a few massive boulders. Soon the trail reaches the cliff base and joins the Short Woodland Carriageway. A glimpse back up the slope reveals the gazebos atop Eagle Cliff. The route turns right and the wide path moves west.

After a few steps, the Short Woodland Carriageway ends at the Humpty Dumpty Carriageway. Again the route goes right (north). The carriageway curves to the west and north, and after a few hundred feet encounters the junction with the blue spur trail to the Giant's Path. Another gazebo, with a great view to the south, adjoins the junction.

The blue spur trail leads to the Giant's Path and Giant's Workshop. The foot trail is more challenging, bouncing up and down on the jumbled ground. Progress remains slow, and planning the next few steps becomes important. Red paint helps mark the route. Sunbaked outcrops alternate with cool, often icy fissures in the chaotic landscape. Footing can be challenging when dry, and dangerous when wet. Small hemlocks, birch, blueberries, mountain laurel and mosses try to colonize any small pocket of soil among the huge boulders. Although nutrients are at a premium, the vegetation that can live in the infertile crevices has unchallenged access to sunlight. In other places, the rocks shade the ground, but retain moisture, providing a different, yet still important benefit to the plants using these niches.

As the trail heads north, it moves from the exposed, rocky outcrops to a well developed oak-hemlock and pine forest. Soils are thicker and the shade is often a welcome umbrella. Travel becomes easier. Unfortunately, the hemlock are under attack from the hemlock woolly adelgid. The insect is easy to see—just turn over a hemlock twig and look for the white fluff at the base of the needles.

This accidentally-introduced pest feeds on the juice flowing to and from a hemlock's needles. The insect secretes a waxy coating to protect itself from predators and dehydration. In order to foil the insect's attack, the hemlock will drop the affected needles. If a hemlock drops its needles for a few years, it depletes the tree's energy reserves. Without new sugar production from its needles, the tree will starve and die within three to five years. There are no practical means for saving an entire forest of adelgid-impacted hemlocks, so it is likely this forest will change dramatically as the new century progresses.

The Humpty Dumpty Path ends at the Giant's Path. The Giant's Path winds down the mountainside, passing through what appears to be a ruined city of huge conglomerate blocks. The area is aptly named the Giant's Workshop, as it does appear that a race of giants might have tried to build something from the angled, jumbled rocks. For those who love the piles of rock that typify the Gunks, this is one of the best areas to experience the characteristics and feel of Shawangunk conglomerate. It is a great place to explore, even though it is out of the way and limits the choices for returning to the hotel grounds.

Upon returning to the trail junction (a moderate climb back up from the Giant's Workshop), the Arched Rocks Path begins and heads northeast. This red-marked trail skirts a fifty-foot cliff wall of conglomerate that arches over the trail in many places. Sounds echo off the curved rock faces. Bird droppings from protected nest sites along the cliff are common. The trail bounces along the cliff base, shaded by a forest mainly of hemlock—a forest threatened by the hemlock woolly adelgid. Look for the many joints and cracks in the conglomerate—the first steps in its eventual destruction by wind, water, sun and ice.

Upon reaching the blue-marked Cathedral Path, the Arched Rocks Path ends. Turn right (west) to re-ascend Eagle Cliff. Oak and pine become more prevalent. The Cathedral Path is a no-nonsense climb back to Copes Lookout—among the best viewpoints on Eagle Cliff. The path jumps and surges up the cliff wall, needling its way through some tight rock formations before merging with the top layers of conglomerate on Eagle Cliff.

Copes Lookout is a Shawangunk highlight. It provides one the most impressive views of the Catskill Mountains from the Gunks. It includes the Wallkill Valley, the Shawangunks as they race south into New Jersey, and the southern and central Catskills. Slide Mountain, the Catskills' highest peak at 4,180 feet, is an easy landmark to spot. Sandwiched between two major valleys, the sounds and sights of civilization are rarely left behind in the Shawangunks, yet the mountains still provide a welcome and unique retreat. A gazebo marks Copes Lookout and shares the ground with a small plaque celebrating the creation of the Mohonk Preserve.

From Copes Lookout there are a variety of routes back to the hotel. All are easy and provide slightly different perspectives of the mountaintop. The Copes Lookout Path is the most direct, lifting onto Eagle Cliff's spine and intersecting the western leg of the Eagle Cliff Carriageway as it approaches the hotel. Along the path are a large number of tree blowdowns, a product of the major winter ice storms that impact the Shawangunks once every few years. New growth quickly moves in to colonize the open ground, but the repeated disturbances make it difficult for a mature forest to re-establish on the infertile, fire-prone slopes.

Returning to the Mountain House brings a fresh understanding of the area. The terrain around the hotel is as much a part of the Mohonk Mountain House experience as the Victorian structure itself. Completing a hike on the hotel grounds is part of a Shawangunk tradition reaching back more than 150 years. Between the great views and an insight on outdoor recreation spanning two centuries, the hike to Eagle Cliff generates memories that will last a lifetime.

# THE TRAPPS AND SKY TOP

Mohonk Mountain House from Sky Top with the Catskills in the background

## Hike: The Trapps and Sky Top

**Distance:** 7.75 miles

**Parking:** Mohonk Preserve Visitor Center off Route 44/55, .4 miles west of the intersection with the western end of NY 299, and 5.0 miles east of the entrance to Minnewaska State Park Preserve. Other parking is available closer to the trailhead, but time restrictions may apply. Trail begins at Trapps Bridge, which crosses the road 1.1 miles west of the visitor center.

**Fees:** $5 per person, Mohonk Preserve. Yearly membership available.

**Difficulty:** Difficult

**Elevation change:** (lowest to highest points on route): 640 feet

**GPS reference points:**

Trail head (Trapps Bridge): 41°45.804' N, 74°09.347' W
Rhododendron Bridge:　41°45.493' N, 74°09.911' W
Smiley Tower on Sky Top: 41°44.210' N, 74°11.066' W

**Details:**

0.00 Trail begins at Trapps Bridge. Cross bridge to Overcliff Carriageway (no markings). Turn left (north). Overcliff Carriageway heads generally northeast.

2.40 Overcliff Carriageway ends at Rhododendron Bridge. Cross bridge and turn left (north) on Oakwood Drive.

2.55 Oakwood Drive ends at Old Minnewaska Carriageway. Turn right (south).

3.45 Turn right (east) on Forest Drive.

3.50 Turn left (north) at Mohonk Spring. Trail heads onto open rocky slope and can be confusing. Head for the large crevice in the cliff face and look for the red-marked trail.

3.55 Climb the crevice (one-way up).

3.60 At the top turn left (follow the signs).

3.85 Sky Top Tower, 1,542 feet. On leaving follow the Sky Top Path downhill (northeast).

4.05 Reach staircase to the Labyrinth. Turn left.

4.10  Turn left on Spring Path (can also follow the Labyrinth).
4.35  Return to Forest Drive at Mohonk Spring. Turn right on
      Forest Drive, then left on Old Minnewaska Carriageway.
      Trace route back to Rhododendron Bridge.
5.40  Cross Rhododendron Bridge. Turn right (south) on
      Undercliff Carriageway.
7.75  Return to Trapps Bridge. End of hike.

If the Shawangunks were said to have a heart, it would be the
Trapps and Sky Top. Massive cliffs and graceful towers mark this landscape renowned by high society, thrill seekers and nature lovers alike.
A hike through these lands presents a cross-section of the many features that give the Gunks their distinctive character. Like most areas in
the range, the hiking is not difficult, although the climb to the Smiley
tower can provide a unique challenge if approached via the Crevice.
This freehand climb is the closest a non-rock climber will get to the
experience of scaling the cliffs and ledges that bring these short,
rugged mountains worldwide notoriety.

While there are many routes that wind around the Lake Mohonk
area, Sky Top is the destination that best encompasses the area and is
the highlight of this hike. With so many people and paths in and
around the hotel grounds, coming to the tower from the Trapps provides a more solitary experience and better reveals the region's natural
highlights. The Trapps themselves make for a unique and pleasant hike
and include paths that are among the engineering achievements of the
nineteenth century. Adding the Sky Top tower makes for a challenging
adventure.

The circuit begins at the Trapps bridge along routes 44/55. The
Trapps' tilted, hard strata boldly rise from the small, glacier-enhanced
gap. The Delaware Indians used this mountain pass as a major war trail.
The Trapps is a Dutch name meaning "staircase," but the name was
actually applied to a small settlement below the cliffs. Imposing ridges
define the Trapps' eastern side, while a gentle bow and then a steep

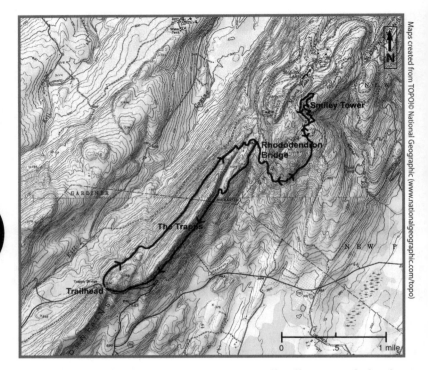

Maps created from TOPO!© National Geographic (www.nationalgeographic.com/topo)

descent deliver the ridgeline to the Coxing Kill Valley. Jagged chunks of white talus are strewn at the base of the rock walls. The steep barrier formed by the Trapps is an excellent place to observe how the Hudson Valley's milder climate impacts the east side of the Shawangunks. In spring the warm air brings an earlier growing season. Wildflowers bloom and leaves emerge earlier. In contrast, fall colors peak about a week later as winter's long fingers reach the western side of the mountains first. Winter's fiercest winds and coldest temperatures remain on the western side of the range.

Options for exploring the area abound, but the most scenic route heads west to the Overcliff Carriageway. The wide, hard-packed trail makes for easy walking. Wildflowers from dainty violets of early spring to purple and white asters that grace the slopes in autumn, add splashes of color.

In autumn the area crawls with millipedes. These hard-bodied, burgundy and orange, tube-like creatures migrate across the paths and crawl about the area in astounding numbers. Some of them reach six inches in length. They lumber along slowly, curling into shielded spirals when threatened. Unfortunately for them, they are no match for stomping feet. Millipedes feast on dead and decaying animals and organic matter. It is not a glamorous lifestyle, but their numbers prove that it is a successful one.

The carriageway curves to the east until locking in a northwesterly course paralleling the Shawangunks' main axis. Carved into the mountain more than 500 feet above the Coxing Kill Valley, which is also known as The Clove, the landscape takes on a rugged, wilderness character. A few glimpses through the tree cover also reveal the Gunks' neighboring ridgeline and its high points: Ronde Barre, Dickie Barre and Rock Hill. The widest of these views includes the highest peaks of the neighboring Catskills.

Slicing through a forest of chestnut oak, black birch, red maple, sassafras, witch hazel, northern red oak, black gum (very red in autumn) and American chestnut, the trail remains level, depending on steep landscape to provide additional views. Although pitch pine and mountain laurel are scattered about the Trapps, they are more common upslope where nutrients and soils are less plentiful. Fire also has been a less common agent in this area. Unlike farther south, where the Gunks level off into wide plateaus, the alternating series of valleys and ridge tops increases the local diversity. Moisture from the streams and seeds can move up the mountain. Temperatures are often more moderate as well.

In areas where small streams cross the carriageway, the surrounding forest changes with the increase in moisture. Grape vines climb and twist about a forest of northern red oak, white ash and hickory. Hemlocks also join the forest showing how the addition of only a small amount of water can have a big impact on the forest community. One benefit of this additional diversity is a richer palette of fall color.

After about 1.75 miles the carriageway leaves the west-facing cliff and begins a series of twists and bends as it works its way east and north. Immediately, the forest character changes as well. Unlike on the exposed cliffs, a multi-layered forest develops. Oak and hickory become more prominent and taller. Stately trunks rise more than fifty feet and their crowns form a solid canopy. Feathery, dark green hemlock becomes a major forest component, a strong contrast with the bright white cliffs. The fire-dependent species so common throughout the range disappear.

The main reason for this change is the rock. The carriageway's base is now Martinsburg shale, a soft rock that underlies the entire Shawangunk ridge. Unable to withstand erosion like its conglomerate neighbor, this dark, thin-layered rock breaks down quickly. Although it cannot support the mountain heights, the eroding shale breaks down to become the foundation for deeper, nutrient-rich soils. Within the Gunks the hard conglomerates capping the range uphold the area's distinct geology, but cannot provide fertile habitats. The opposite is true of the shales, presenting a defining dichotomy in the Shawangunks' natural history.

The next major landmark is the Rhododendron Bridge, an example of deceptive advertising. People coming for the rhododendron will be disappointed—there are none to be found. At the wooden bridge a network of trails and carriageways merge, including the Undercliff Road, the return route back to the main highway. Rhododendron Bridge is a simple structure crossing a small stream and wetland forest. Black birch, a tree known for its strong wintergreen smell, is common. A wintergreen tea can be brewed by boiling the twigs after stripping their outer bark.

The route to the tower crosses the small wooden bridge, and then turns left (north) onto the Old Minnewaska Carriageway. The path becomes steeper, a bit more of a challenge than Overcliff Carriageway. The forest remains rooted in the deeper, richer soils. Underscoring this change is the presence of sugar maple, an uncommon tree within the

Looking southwest along the Gunks from Sky Top

Gunks. The climb delivers the trail to an open view to the south. In the foreground rise the Trapps' steep cliffs. The view continues to stretch south, following the Gunks' eastern edge. Once past the mass of Millbrook Mountain, it becomes harder to see individual points, but the eye can wander down to the obelisk topping High Point in New Jersey, more than thirty miles distant.

The Old Minnewaska Carriageway curves around a mountain promontory, slowly altering its bearing from southeast to northeast. Then it joins with a series of routes that weave a confusing web of carriageways and trails. The route to Sky Top continues along the main path, requiring a turn to the right (east) at Laurel Ledge Carriageway. The forest remains lush, full and inviting, a healthy collection of deciduous and conifer trees not limited by poor soil and a lack of water. Signs of man's influence on the land become apparent. Norway spruce, a European species planted to reforest open slopes, stand in orderly rows. Up on Eagle Cliff, west of the trail, a gazebo perches atop the exposed rock face. Open fields also appear, revealing the low form of Illinois Mountain across the Wallkill Valley.

A deer browse-line shows in the field—a sign of overpopulation. When deer become too common, they alter the balance of the forest and become a threat to themselves, the local natural community and humans. With their primary natural predator, gray wolves, extirpated (extinct within the region), deer have thrived. They can alter forest composition and damage crops because they prefer to eat specific plants, such as sugar maple, various wildflowers and agricultural crops. In terms of the forest, this reduces the ability of certain species to replace themselves. With so many deer surviving, they become prone to disease, and in winter, starvation. The deer populations are less healthy than if the herd was culled, either by natural predators or humans.

After a couple of more intersections, the carriageway intersects Forest Drive. Turn left (east) and head downhill through a hemlock forest. Through the trees, the bright blue sky and brighter bleached cliffs of Sky Top show through the myriad of shadowy needles. The tower and cliff are so striking that they make it easy to miss the quick turn at Mohonk Spring. The small, stone and wood structure is a pleasant spot. A thin trail slides along the soft dirt and needle-lined ground. Hard to follow in places, it quickly leads to a ring of barren talus. Once on the rocks, it is difficult to follow a specific trail to the looming 200-foot rock wall. At first glance the vertical formation appears impossible to climb. The only imperfection in the massive block of rock is a small crevice—a dark line among the light stone. This feature, The Crevice, is the route. At the wall's base is a red-marked trail that leads to the dark slice, but any route to the opening will suffice.

Once at the opening, the true nature of moving through and up this rock wall becomes apparent. Ranging from four to six feet wide, The Crevice is not for those afraid of heights or tight places. Wooden ladders and stairs assist the climb through the imposing rock cliffs. Part caving, part rock-climbing, this is about as close as it comes to experiencing these activities without donning special equipment. The ascent is a unique opportunity to get "inside" the Shawangunks. Cool air spills from the sheltered space. To prevent long delays and accidents, The Crevice is designated one-way (up).

Once through the main slot, the trail emerges on an open rock ledge with views. The wind is often much stronger on this high, exposed ground. Shawangunk conglomerate again tiles the ground, and the forest reverts to a stiff set of pitch pine, mountain laurel and blueberries. To the west is Eagle Cliff and the outflow from Lake Mohonk. Also to the west are the southern and central Catskills. To the south, following the Shawangunk ridge, are Millbrook Mountain and the set of communication towers by Lake Maratanza, marking the Gunks' highest point. Farther south, in New Jersey, High Point's distinct obelisk spears the sky. To the southeast is the deep gap where the Hudson River cuts through the Hudson Highlands.

From the ledge a short footpath heads west, circling the stone watchtower and then overlooking Lake Mohonk. Then, the path to the tower opens. The current eighty-foot tower is the third structure built on the site. Named for Albert K. Smiley, the tower is a memorial to him, his efforts at Mohonk, and his humanitarianism. Before this area was bought by the Smiley family, its place names were much more mundane. Sky Top was known as Paltz Point, and Lake Mohonk was Paltz Pond.

The tower was also built to help spot fires, a constant threat to the hotel and surrounding area. Started in 1921 and completed in 1923, the curent tower reflects the graceful, soaring gothic revival of the roaring '20s. Since its opening, hotel guests and other hikers have come to this elevated perch like a moth to flame, all attracted to this lone beacon and its magnificent vista.

The tower base sits at 1,542 feet. Once inside, sunlight gives way to heavy shadow. The stone tower is cold and drafty except on summer's hottest days, when the cool air is a welcome relief. The body's cooling systems have a hard time adjusting to the abrupt shift in conditions. Once the toll in footsteps is paid, the stairs emerge onto an open viewing platform hosting a spectacular, wide-ranging view. Unhampered by tree or mountain, high winds often stream along the observation deck, howling and screaming though the stonework's open spaces.

The 360-degree panorama includes, to the west, most of the Catskills. Grouped into two sets of high peaks, the northern ridgeline

Smiley Tower on Sky Top

is dominated by the Devil's Path and 4,040-foot Hunter Mountain. Along the Catskills' eastern escarpment, and visible from here, was the Catskill Mountain House, the region's premier resort of the 1800s. The view here once spanned from one great hotel to another, but only the Mohonk Mountain House survived to see the twenty-first century.

The Mountain House sits just beyond the deep blue waters of Lake Mohonk, its Victorian turrets and gray stone walls an impressive sight among the mountain splendor. The hotel was started in 1870 by Albert Smiley, and has remained in the family ever since. Through the decades the hotel and grounds expanded. The hotel itself reached its current size by 1910, with the last major edition being the stone towers that dominate the hotel's current profile. Over the years the Mountain House has hosted many important politicians, including Presidents Hayes, Wilson and Taft, together with business leaders, conservationists and spiritual men, but it was from hosting a series of Indian conferences in the early 1900s that the hotel and Smiley family gained national recognition. More recently the exterior was used as the setting for the 1992 film, *The Road to Wellville*. Always interested in conservation and quality-of-life issues, and facing the crunch of increasing taxes and tougher business conditions, in 1963 the Smiley family detached 5,300 acres to form the Mohonk Trust. The hotel retains another 2,200 acres.

To the north the Shawangunk ridge dwindles as it falls into the Hudson Valley. Immediately below the tower is a reflecting pool created from the quarry used for the tower's stone. The pool holds 1.2 million gallons of water and is kept ready for use in fighting fires. Beyond the reflecting pool is a larger body of water that serves as the hotel's reservoir.

Far to the northeast rise Vermont's Green Mountains, visible only on the best of days. Massachusetts' highest points, Mount Greylock (3,429 feet) and Mount Everett (2,600 feet), are easier to see. The view also stretches into Connecticut and spies the Taconic Mountains, Hudson Highlands and Plattekill Hills before the eye returns to the Shawangunks as they race south into New Jersey.

Sky Top is the setting for Sanford Gifford's painting, *Shawangunk Mountains*, a subtly colored, oval-shaped painting completed in 1854 before Mohonk was even a name. Still referred to as Paltz Point at the time, only a small tavern house run by a local farmer existed in this spot. Gifford records the view south from Sky Top. The Near Trapps, Trapps and Millbrook Mountain are profiled against a cloudy sky. The scene does not show any sign of development, but the landscape does not appear as a rugged wilderness, either. Unlike the Catskills, which set the standard for American landscape artists in the mid-1800s, the Shawangunks were mostly ignored.

Since the Crevice is a one-way route, the return to Mohonk Spring and Rhododendron Bridge offers a chance to get a better look at the Mohonk Mountain House. Heading west and north along Sky Top, the wide carriageway heads for another rugged path, the Labyrinth. Stationed above the Mountain House and lake, the route provides many fine views of the resort. Adding to the scene's mountainous character, the Catskills rise beyond the Rondout Valley. A few gazebos, part of the resort experience of the Mountain House, are set alongside the carriageway.

Since there are so many paths in the area around Lake Mohonk, it can be difficult to remain oriented. On the other hand, most of the trails intersect or are in sight of one another, making it easy to find a parallel route back toward Mohonk Spring. At the first trail intersection a cut-over to the Labyrinth intersects the carriageway from the left (west). Following the small path, it bounds down a set of rock stairs to complete the descent from Sky Top's cliffs. At the bottom of the stairs, the route to Mohonk Spring via the Labyrinth Path heads left (south). The route curves along the cliff wall, its shade and the moisture from the lake supporting a thick forest of small hemlocks. The Spring Path parallels the Labyrinth, but is a little lower down the mountainside. Either route is fine.

As the trails curve around the protruding nub of Sky Top, it remains in sight of the Lake Shore Carriageway, which intersects Forest Road. Once back at the spring house, the return route to Rhododendron Bridge follows the same route used to approach the area. The hammering sounds of the downy woodpeckers are common. Look for their black, white and red bodies stationed among the trees

Mohonk Mountain House from Sky Top

and flying to their favorite perches. Besides drilling for food, this woodpecker also drills into softer areas of trees to hollow out a cavity for its nests. With so much energy used to create a nest, most wood-peckers will aggressively defend their nesting site.

A number of exposed formations of Martinsburg shale are appar-ent in this area. Another of the gaps in the Shawangunks, this point adds to the area's rugged appearance. The weak rock continues to erode, breaking easily from even small amounts of pressure. As the weak rock is broken and carried away, it undermines the support need-ed by the harder conglomerate.

Once across Rhododendron Bridge, the Undercliff Carriageway heads southwest (left) from the intersection. Moving through an area of scrub trees and shrubs, the carriageway makes a few sharp turns as it approaches the Trapps. The trail crosses a small stream filled with skunk cabbage, a plant known for its distinctive smell when stems or leaves are broken. Skunk cabbage also has the unique ability to pro-duce heat, allowing its first spring shoots to melt remaining ice and snow at the start of the season. Flowering early, the skunk cabbage's warm microenvironment attracts insects, which in turn visit other skunk cabbages, thus pollinating this species.

Once at the foot of the cliffs, the trail heads southwest and remains straight for more than a mile. The forest here is well-established and healthy. The massive Trapps wall protects the nearby forest by shelter-ing the trees from winter's winds and slowing water loss. The diversi-ty of trees and their size is impressive. Sugar maple, uncommon throughout the Gunks, grows well here. In areas with sun exposure, staghorn sumac works to fill the gaps. The small, spreading sumac's red berries can be brewed into a lemony tea.

The cliff walls are impressive, also. This is the heart of the Shawangunks' famous rock-climbing area. Many trails wind their way through the talus slopes to the base of the cliff where climbing begins. The sounds of metal against metal, and metal against rock are common. Ropes and climbers often add splotches of color to the light gray wall.

Just as impressive as the rock walls and limited view of the neigh-boring Wallkill Valley is the construction of the carriageway itself.

Built in the late 1800s by hand, construction costs were more than $1 per foot, an expensive price for that time. Rocks and boulders were moved or crushed. Surfaces were filled and leveled. Working with only simple tools and on such chaotic ground to create such a strong and enduring pathway is a feat of quality engineering and workmanship impressive even by today's standards.

Well before returning to the road, traffic noise, first from Route 299, then from Routes 44/55 zooms up the mountain, accompanying the trail until its end. Once reaching Routes 44/55, the trail takes a sharp right (west) before ending at the Trapps Bridge and the Overcliff Carriageway.

# MILLBROOK MOUNTAIN

**Hike: Millbrook Mountain**

**Distance:** 5.65 miles

**Parking:** Mohonk Preserve Visitor Center off Route 44/55, .4 miles west of the intersection with the western end of NY 299, and 5.0 miles east of the entrance to Minnewaska State Park Preserve. Other parking is available closer to the trailhead, but time restrictions may apply. Trail begins at Trapps Bridge, which crosses the road 1.1 miles west of the visitor center.

**Fees:** $5 per person, Mohonk Preserve. Yearly membership available.

**Difficulty:** Difficult

**Elevation change:** (lowest to highest points on route): 600 feet

**GPS reference points:**

Trail head (Trapps Bridge): 41°45.804' N, 74°09.347' W
Millbrook Mountain (junction with Millbrook Mountain Trail):                 41°45.493' N, 74°09.911' W

**Details:**

0.00 Start at Trapps Bridge on Trapps Carriageway and turn left (southwest).

0.05 Turn left (southeast) on the Millbrook Ridge Trail.

0.75 Pass Bayards Path.

1.95 Pass Millbrook Cross Trail.

2.75 Reach eastern crest of Millbrook Mountain, 1,605 feet. Look for red-marked, Millbrook Mountain Trail and take a right (northwest).

2.95 Turn right (northeast) on to Coxing Trail.

4.60 Coxing Trail ends at Trapps Carriageway. Turn right (northeast).

5.65 Return to Trapps Bridge. End of hike.

Millbrook Mountain is the closest the Shawangunks have to a landform that looks like a mountain. Although it only rises to 1,820 feet, its sharp, dramatic, 1,605-foot eastern crest is an imposing site. Millbrook Mountain's eastern face is a sheer cliff of 600 feet. From the Wallkill Valley the mountain appears cleaved in half, its cross section a classic anticline. The exposed mountainside looks like a huge geologic map.

Rocky and studded with pitch pines, the harsh terrain magnifies the area's mountainous character. The hike is one of the Gunks' most distinctive, offering spectacular and unique scenery. In addition, the route visits some of the region's most striking contrasts in habitat and ecosystems. If there was only time for one excursion in the Gunks, the trip to Millbrook Mountain would be a top choice.

The trail begins where the Trapps Carriageway crosses Routes 44/55 on a steel bridge, the sturdy overpass symbolic of the care and quality invested into the region's many carriageways. Heading left (southwest) from the intersection, the carriageway reaches a trail junction after about fifty feet. Marked with blue paint, The Millbrook Ridge Trail heads left (southeast) from the carriageway. Immediately, the trail hops onto the exposed conglomerates capping most of the Shawangunk ridge. The trail lifts steeply, leaping and bouncing its way up the rough boulders and outcrops. Tilted by past mountain-building events, the rocks lean at an angle. Sometimes this provides for great footholds, but in other spots it makes travel difficult. In most places the rocks are rough and provide good footing, while other, smooth surfaces reveal their recent glacial encounters. Highly polished and covered by finely etched parallel lines and chattermarks, the slow-to-erode conglomerate preserves much of its recent geologic history.

The trail uses its first few hundred steps to reach a set of east-facing cliffs, The Near Trapps. The high cliffs, popular with rock climbers, are typical of the Gunks' rugged nature. Once atop this mountain backbone, views open to the west and north. To the west rise the Catskills' soft, glacially rounded shapes. Most prominent among the distant peaks are the Devil's Path mountains and High Point. To the north and in the western foreground, eyes can travel along Shawangunk ridges.

The neighboring ridge to the west is part of Minnewaska State Park Preserve. To the north lie the Trapps, the center of the area's famed rock climbing. The small valley between the Trapps and Near Trapps formed in an old fault line, the broken rock less resistant to erosion. The trail continues southwest along this mountain backbone, presenting views of the Catskills, including some of its highest peaks—Westkill and Hunter mountains.

Between the hard rock and steep slopes, there is little opportunity for soils to develop or accumulate. In many places the earth is barren, while in more sheltered cracks a thin soil, sandy and infertile, lightly coats the land. Not many plants can grow here, but pitch pine is a notable exception, its genetic machinery adapted for the harsh conditions. Twisted and broken by high winds and ice, these sharp-needled, sticky trees provide a semblance of forest cover. Like the famous Joshua trees of the American southwest, these living sculptures produce imaginative shapes and lines. Each tree has a personality all its own. Between the rock, pitch pine and spent needles, the landscape displays a tricolor of yellow-green, white and copper—a unique forest environment by any standard.

Soon the trail crests the ridge upholding the Shawangunks' eastern front. To the east the land falls away as the topography dives down the Near Trapps into the Wallkill Valley. Along a more gentle route, the main road, Routes 44/55, snakes its way between the gap separating the Trapps and Near Trapps. New Paltz and its university campus are easy-to-find landmarks within the valley. Cottonwoods line the riverbank, well-adapted for this flood-prone area. In a land of south-flowing rivers, the Wallkill is the exception, its waters heading north from New Jersey to merge with the Rondout Creek at Rosendale, and then continuing north to the Hudson River. In another quirk of geography, when the river meets the lower-volume, shorter creek, the combined watercourse takes on the creek's name before spilling into the Hudson River at Kingston.

Across the Wallkill Valley rise the Plattekill Mountains, anchored by the 1,129-foot Illinois Mountain, home to a number of communication towers. Farther south are the Hudson Highlands—represented by

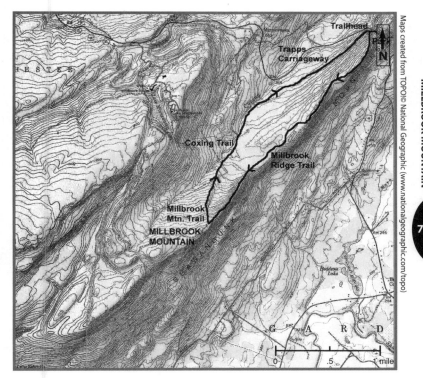

Maps created from TOPO!© National Geographic (www.nationalgeographic.com/topo)

Mount Beacon, Breakneck Mountain, and Storm King—and the Hudson Valley. Along the eastern horizon, the Taconics stretch into Connecticut and Massachusetts. Compared with the forested, rugged and mountainous scenes to the west and north, the view east is gentle and pastoral.

Bounded on its eastern side by a 200-foot drop, the trail demands attention as it continues to push southwestward along a knife-edge of rock topping the ridge. Jagged, irregular contours define the route. The open platform provides some glimpses of the wide Wallkill Valley to the east and the tight, sheltered valley of the Coxing Kill to the west. All along the cliff, broken pieces of the ridge litter the wall's base. Most of the fallen slabs date to just after the continental ice sheet retreated, when freezing and thawing events were more prevalent. As water seeps into joints and freezes, it expands, forcing the rock further apart. When it melts, the rock rebounds. The process continues, repeating itself day after day, year after year, until the rock yields.

The Shawangunks make a strong border in terms of climate, separating the milder Hudson Valley from the cooler conditions prevailing in the Catskills and the rest of upstate New York. In this region the differences in temperature—especially winter lows and length of growing season—and moisture favor forest associations typically found in warmer areas. To the east, below the sharp cliffs of the eastern Gunks, the mountains shelter the forests, keeping the trees green longer in the fall and favoring earlier spring growth. The effect is further enhanced by the southeast-facing slopes, concentrating the sunlight and warmth.

Slanted to the east, the Shawangunks' rock faces are steeper along their eastern front since this side of the mountains was closer to the continental collisions shaping North America's east coast. Locations to the east generally rose more than those to the west. Glacially plucked, scoured and polished, the eastern edge of this ridge has become a sheer cliff. Atop the cliff, where little soil or moisture remains long, pitch pine, blueberries, huckleberries, bear oak and red maple cover the slopes. Most of these species are specialized to handle poor soil fertility, low moisture conditions and fire.

In autumn the blueberry and huckleberry leaves turn a deep crimson, providing a new set of contrasts with the yellow-green needles, dark tree trunks, copper needle carpet and white conglomerate. Like ornaments, a few yellow, red and bronze maple and oak leaves lie among the berries and pitch pines. The scene takes on a Christmas-like appearance. With the Gunks often mired in snow and ice during the winter holiday season, fall is often the best time to experience the Gunks' version of holiday cheer.

Lifting on Bayards Ridge, the trail encounters its first intersection. The half-mile Bayards Path breaks off to the northwest, while the red-marked trail leads back to the Trapps Carriageway. To the east are the Bayards, the cliffs providing the area and the trail its name. The rock

The profile of Millbrook Mountain from the north gives it
the appearance of a rugged crest.

face is popular among rock climbers. Continuing to head south along the ridge, the Millbrook Ridge Trail keeps its gentle rise.

With an explosion of sound, wing beats fill the air. Ruffed grouse nest and feed in these woods, but they often wait until a potential predator gets close before flying away in a flurry of activity. In a rush of chaotic movement, they hope to startle any potential predator, using the time to fly to safety. Coyotes, bobcats and humans are the biggest threats to ruffed grouse. The two-pound bird is a favorite among hunters.

Colored in muted shades of brown, ruffed grouse blend well with the forest floor. The name "ruffed" comes from the bird's long, shiny, black or chocolate-colored neck feathers, which are more prominent on the male. When in full display, either in defense of territory or showing off for a hen, these feathers extend into a spectacular ruff. Combined with a fully fanned tail, this display makes the bird appear twice as large as it is. The male grouse proclaims his property rights through a drumming display, a sound familiar to most people spending time in the woods. The sound forms when a male beats his wings against the air to create a vacuum, generating sound in the same way lightning generates thunder.

When the ground is free of snow, ruffed grouse feed on a wide variety of green leaves, fruits and some insects. Occasionally, they eat snakes, frogs and salamanders as well. When snow covers the ground, as it does for most of the winter across most of their range, the grouse eat tree buds or catkins from aspen, birch, cherry and ironwood.

As the trail climbs, it begins to afford more extensive views to the southeast and south. The highlights include West Point and the Hudson Highlands. A large expanse of greenbrier, a thorny climbing vine, produces an odd picture frame. On most days, the brown haze tinting the atmosphere is higher to the southeast, a direct result of the New York metropolitan area's air pollution. In the summer this haze often builds into the Hudson Valley and Shawangunks, swallowing the distant mountains and blurring the closer landforms.

Escorting the trail through this area are knuckles of light-colored rock. Running in long lines parallel to the ridge, the protruding rocks look like a miniature mountain range. Rusty piles of discarded needles fill the areas between the light gray rocks. Small gaps and cliffs, most formed from jointing, complete the broken ground. The level path retains this flavor until reaching another climb.

The trail rises onto a promontory with a view to the south. Still almost a mile away, Millbrook Mountain surges more than 500 feet into the sky—by far the Shawangunks' most impressive-looking rise. The craggy, jagged peak is an imposing sight, in many ways more akin to landforms in Utah than New York. The exposed, harsh mountaintop seems the perfect place for a fairy tale castle, complete with pitch pine guards on all the rocky outlooks. The mountain's eastern edge is a sheer cliff, and a look down the 900-foot wall awaits those reaching the top.

Although Millbrook Mountain appears to crest as a sharp peak, the profile is one-sided and deceptive, as the mountaintop actually grades onto a wider plateau. The bold outline presents an uphill challenge, among the Gunks' more impressive ascents. Adding to the mountain's fierce landscape are the angular rocks and spiky pitch pines. In contrast, the foreground drops into a softer-looking forest before lifting to climb Millbrook Mountain's profile.

The trail then twists its way through a series of rivulets and small valleys. As soon as the trail begins to descend, the land retains more moisture and is shaded for longer periods of time. The air becomes cooler and damper. In the depression, downed leaves compete with needles for the dominant ground cover. Hemlock becomes a key species, along with black gum. In autumn black gums display intense reds. Tree size increases, especially among the hemlock. Pitch pines, able to thrive where other trees cannot grow, drop out of the forest, unable to compete in the richer, thicker soils. Bird life becomes more apparent as well, with juncos, woodpeckers and chickadees flitting though the trees.

The path crosses a small stream valley, an area often wet, or at least muddy. Most of the rest of the trail will be bone dry. Overall, the area feels like an oasis. Unlike the open, dry forests lining most of the ridge, the layered, wetter forests here provide a cool, comfortable retreat. The area is also better protected from the wind. As the trail moves through this wetter, sheltered area, it passes the Millbrook Cross Path, a short trail that heads right (west) down to the Coxing Trail.

Before beginning the uphill push to reach Millbrook Mountain, the trail passes through a pleasant forest of chestnut oak, northern red oak and red maple, filled with an understory of blueberries. Without any taller shrubs clogging the understory, it is easy to see along the forest floor, giving the woods a more inviting, open feel.

One last twist brings the trail to the mountain's final incline. A dark hemlock stand, littered with white conglomerate boulders, escorts the trail away from the precipitous drop along the mountain's eastern edge. The climb is the trail's most difficult challenge, often tracing a knife-like backbone of rock. Pitch pine again become the dominant vegetation, and views begin to build to the north, a more impressive overview of the area seen from atop the Near Trapps at the route's beginning. The view keeps building as elevation increases. Sky Top, Eagle Cliff and the Barres create the foreground, with a large slice of the

The Trapps from the Near Trapps

Catskills in the distance. To the west is the higher Shawangunk ridge, holding Lake Minnewaska and Beacon Hill.

Millbrook Mountain is not only challenging, it is also deceiving. Many false summits psychologically extend the route. What appears to be the summit becomes only an open ridge or a small level area. Soon, views to the south open again to reveal the Wallkill Valley, Hudson Highlands and Taconic Mountains. Then, in another deceiving move, the trail is pushed to the west and continues to climb. A massive rock outcrop hems in the path's eastern side. All traces of the view disappear. A thick covering of hemlock and pitch pine enclose the trail to the west and eclipse the sky. Compared to the open views seen only a few steps ago, the mountaintop seems lost in a subterranean world.

Soon the trail emerges from this odd scene and reaches Millbrook Mountain's most conspicuous peak. The actual summit rises to the west and is about 220 feet higher than this peak, but is a much less spectacular place. From this 1,605-foot peak, a rock ledge stands to the east. Slanted sharply to the west, the ledge is more of a fence. Below this rock hedge, the land plunges 400 feet as a sheer drop—one of the deepest in the eastern United States. At the bottom is a wide ribbon of rock desert, talus lost from the cliff face, mostly in the freezing and thawing so common after the retreat of the last great ice sheet. The topography continues to fall quickly, losing another 500 feet before leveling. The view is open to the north, east and south, but it is the cliff face immediately below that makes this spot so impressive. A few dwarfed, almost bonsai, pitch pines cling to life on the cliff face.

Even here the mountain continues to deceive as the trail moves higher, but now it becomes apparent that the word "summit" is misleading, as the land levels into a wide plateau. Views continue to open to the east, west and north. To the west rises the higher ridge sustaining Minnewaska and Beacon Hill. Pitch pine again dominate the land, this area akin to the Badlands associated with much of the Shawangunks' southern half.

Located a few feet away from the cliff face is the red-marked Millbrook Mountain Trail, which begins the loop back to Routes 44/55. The trail, which heads immediately downhill (left), can be tricky to find among the almost uniform vegetation of pitch pine, mountain laurel and blueberries. In autumn the blueberry plants' red leaves are a poignant reminder of the fires set to keep the area's berry crop strong. Shallow soils cover the land, except on the path, where water and feet have worn them away. As the trail descends, it provides a nice overview of the Coxing Kill Valley.

After only a few minutes of walking, the trail hits the blue-marked Coxing Trail, which heads to the northeast (right). Once on the Coxing Trail, it reveals a look back to the Millbrook ridgeline and extends the view north to Sky Top, Eagle Cliff and the Catskills. Directly east rises the sharp uplift of Millbrook Mountain. The trail is uneven and deceiving, placing feet and mind on alert. Many rock cairns help guide the way, but randomly placed rocks are prevalent and can make finding cairns difficult, especially at twilight. As the trail descends, soils thicken and pitch pines begin to yield the ground to oaks and maples. Many of the oaks are only wooden ghosts, victims of the gypsy moth.

As the valley grows and the water supply becomes more reliable, the forest community undergoes sweeping changes. The land becomes greener as nutrients and water become plentiful and the valley walls provide shelter from wind and ice. Pines give way to hardwoods. American chestnut sprouts join the forest. Red maple, which grows on all but the poorest of sites, accent the land in spring and fall. Tulip poplars, American beech, sugar maple and hemlock also grow here.

As the streams become larger and the valley becomes wider, the poor drainage results in forested wetlands. In places, the path becomes so waterlogged that a boardwalk elevates the trail. In drier areas, the trail is better graded, growing into a mountain expressway. Tree size increases and the wind retreats. The whole landscape takes on a more tranquil atmosphere. Deer frequent the area and carve a distinct browse line five feet above the ground. Few trees have leaves lower than this line—those trying become deer food. Bird chatter fills the air, especially in the morning and evening.

The Coxing Trail then spills onto the Trapps Carriageway. Heading east (left), the carriage road is another step closer to civilization—a mountain superhighway compared to the trek's other routes. The car-

Jack-in-the-pulpit can grow beneath a variety of wet and dry woodlands.
In late summer, the plant displays a bright cluster of red berries.

riageway parallels Routes 44/55, but it is almost a mile until they cross at the Trapps Bridge. The carriageway is pinched between the ridgeline and the road. Dead trees, many oaks killed by the gypsy moth, line the path. Along the carriageway the forest becomes more typical of the Gunks: black gum, oaks, and birches. On completing the journey the trail curves to the east and sights the Trapps Bridge. The Millbrook Ridge Trail is off to the east (right). The bridge marks the end of the hike.

Millbrook Mountain is the ultimate Shawangunk cliff, but it also offers much in the way of scenic views and forest contrasts. Although the hike does not rise to astounding heights, the route is taxing on mind and body. After experiencing the sheer drops, tasty berries, steep climbs, sheltered stream valleys, sharp pitch pines, soft hemlocks, rough rocks and gentle forests, it is no wonder that this land of contrasts provides such an intense and enjoyable experience.

# MINNEWASKA

MINNEWASKA

83

Lake Minnewaska

# THREE FALLS AND HIGH PETERS KILL

Between the Gunks' conglomerate-topped ridges nestle a series of steep, shaded valleys. Often enhanced by weaknesses from jointing and faulting, these creases frequently harbor communities and landscapes strikingly different from the dry, sun-blasted ecosystems topping the infertile ridge tops. Still, the conglomerates do not give way easily, and the streams must work for many years to eat into the hard bedrock. One result is the steep streambeds punctuated with cascades and waterfalls. Some of the most impressive of these falls—Awosting, Sheldon and Peters Kill—lie along the Peters Kill as it works its way northeast to the Rondout Valley.

Hemmed in by a 400-foot canyon, the isolated valley is a fertile haven filled with hemlock, oaks, beech, birch and maple. Dampness clings to the air, rocks and wood. The damp ground muffles sound and provides a gentle padding. Moving up the cliff along the valley's western side to the High Peters Kill Ridge presents an entirely different environment. The land is sunnier, drier and windier. Although less hearty than the pitch pine and blueberry-dominated ridge to the east, the stout oaks, birch and accompanying grasses are much more drought-resistant than the forests in the canyon.

Exploring this area provides an experience full of variety. In some places moisture seems to seep from dense hemlocks stands, while only a few paces away, dry brown grasses break and crunch with each step. Much of the forest community is a blend of the warmer ecosystems found in the Hudson Valley and the cooler climes blanketing the Catskills. Few of the forest associations are classic—neither the climate nor the space is constant enough to promote one forest type over another.

The route—downstream along the Peters Kill and then up the High Peters Kill Ridge before returning to the trail—begins in the lower parking area of Lake Minnewaska Park Preserve. The parking lot is a quarter-mile west of the main entrance. The route begins along the dirt road used to access the parking area, downstream and parallel to the

## Hike: Three Falls and High Peters Kill

**Distance:** 3.40 miles

**Parking:** Lower lot of Minnewaska State Park Preserve, located along Route 44/55, 5.4 miles west of the intersection with the western end of NY 299 and 5.9 miles east of the intersection of route US 209 and Route 44/55.

**Fees:** $5 per car at Minnewaska State Park Preserve. Yearly pass available.

**Difficulty:** Moderate, with one difficult off-trail stretch

**Elevation change:** (lowest to highest points on route): 380 feet

**GPS reference points:**

Parking area:      41°44.102' N, 74°14.673' W
Lowest point (Peters Kill foot bridge):
                41°44.673' N, 74°13.198' W

## Details:

0.00  Start by following road east from parking area. Pass entrance kiosk, cross the Peters Kill, then make an immediate left (east) onto the carriageway paralleling the stream.

0.45  Awosting Falls.

0.85  Carriageway veers left. Leave the carriageway and cross Route 44/55.

0.90  Carefully work down the slope of the north side of the road to reach Sheldon Falls.

1.05  Pass ruins of power plant. Follow the stream down slope until reaching red-marked trail above Peters Kill Falls. Take the trail's left (lower) branch.

1.25  Peters Kill Falls. Continue on red-marked trail.

1.85  Red-marked trail ends at blue-marked High Peters Kill Trail. Turn left (west), cross the bridge and climb the ridge.

2.05  End of steep incline.

3.35  Trail rejoins Route 44/55 just west of the parking area. Turn right.

3.40  Parking area. End of hike.

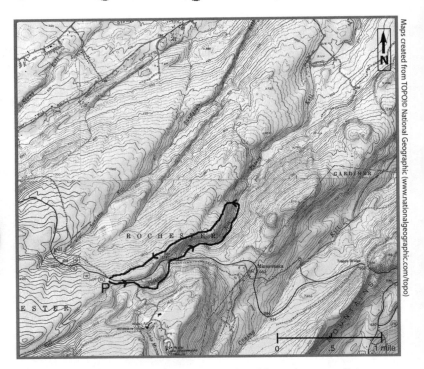

Maps created from TOPO!© National Geographic (www.nationalgeographic.com/topo)

Peters Kill. The flat road provides a comfortable and easy walking surface. The relatively deep and fertile soils support a forest of sugar maple, beech, birch and hemlock. Once past the main entrance, the route crosses the water and slips into the woods (left).

As soon as the blue-marked High Peters Kill Trail heads into the forest, the Peters Kill adds cool moisture to the surrounding air. A thick, hemlock-dominated forest nestles against the trail. A few birch and mountain laurel round out the forest. The carriageway parallels the stream until reaching the top of Awosting Falls. The plunging water resonates with a deep bass. Unlike the water, the trail cannot plunge down the cliff wall; instead, a steep downhill route winds along the rock wall before delivering the carriageway back to the streambed.

Moisture clings and drips to the broken rock structures, encouraging lichens and mosses to grow beneath the hemlock-shrouded slopes.

The trail provides a great view of the forty-foot plunge. Nearly horizontal layers of white and buff-colored rock lie like masonry. A few hemlock and oak branches hang over the stream. Throughout most of the year, the fall is well endowed with water. In winter a thick fog can fill the small natural amphitheater, and in summer the cool water doubles as natural air conditioning. The setting is cool and shadowy, the forest muted by the myriad of spent evergreen needles. Together these slender cast-offs collect on the forest floor to make a copper carpet. After leaving the falls, the carriageway drifts downstream, slowly marking time with the streambed.

The next major landmark appears when the carriageway encounters Routes 44/55. The carriageway veers east and does not cross the road, but the stream's loyalty to gravity continues to pull it down, and the water bubbles with anticipation as it nears the impressive falls and cascades just beyond the road. While the Peters Kill flows easily beneath a bridge, humans need to work their way across the road and then head down a steep slope to reunite with the stream. Although there are some informal trails down to the falls, all of them require caution. The plunge down the wooded slope quickly returns to the streambed. A few hardy trees jut into the sky, having found niches among the rock wall's ledges and cracks. Once in the clove, higher humidity and the sound of rushing water fill the air.

Sheldon Falls holds the head of the clove and has helped carve the impressive canyon. The falls' upper section is a fanning cascade with many pleasant sun-warmed rock ledges. Lying out among the heated rocks and cool spray from the falls makes for perfect napping. Except in the dead of winter, the water never rests, flowing playfully downstream. Next, the water accelerates through a tight flume and surges over a ledge before plunging into a crystal pool. The water then races downhill, gathering the intermittent waters of a tributary leaping from the High Peters Kill Ridge.

As Sheldon Falls comes to a close, it leaps another series of small cliffs. The ruins of an old power plant mar this scene. After so much work to scale the cliffs and work into the isolated valley, the stone building and trestles remaining here are an ugly and unwelcome nuisance among the recovering forest. Built in 1924 to power the Minnewaska mountain houses, the plant was designed to burn coal. When there were shortages of coal during the Great Depression and World War II, the power plant consumed wood. Despite the obvious irony today, the Smiley family, owners of the mountain houses, in an effort to limit air pollution used only hard coal, the cleanest burning coal available at that time. The power plant remained in operation until the late 1950s, when Central Hudson Gas & Electric Corp. began supplying the mountain houses with power.

The waterfall's influence continues beyond the power plant, as it fills the air with sound and moisture. Wetlands and muck are common. A well-developed bottomland forest of hemlock, maple, beech and oak shades the area, corraling even more moisture. Without a formal trail, the stream provides the best guidance. Unmarked trails braid the area, but by remaining close to the stream, there is less chance of becoming disoriented. In addition, there are many chances to cross the mossy stream. Each bank offers its own opportunities for progress and occasions for challenge. In some places, especially along the western side, the high conglomerate cliffs nestle against the water. A short, but steep slope, filled with tangles of roots weaves along the eastern bank. Even though the forest remains lush, a look upslope reveals the drier, harsher conditions where the soils are shallower and there is less moisture for vegetation. Mountain laurel, chestnut oak and blueberries seem to peer jealously over the richer habitats.

The next major feature along the stream is Peters Kill Falls. The playful cataract is more cascade than fall, and is much less impressive than Sheldon Falls. Wide, flat rock platforms provide many opportunities for sun-bathing and photography. The area is often crowded as there is easy access from a parking area along Routes 44/55.

The former ski trails, open habitat and nearby forest cover make excellent habitat for many bird species. Among the most prominent is the rufous-sided towhee. This medium-sized songbird, about the size of a robin but not as fat, makes its distinctive "drink your tea-ea-ea" call

Sheldon Falls

almost relentlessly. The female is brown above, with orange-brown sides and a white belly, while the male sports a hangman's black hood above, with orange-brown sides and white belly. Clearly visible when the bird flies are flashes of white on its wing and tail feathers.

Towhees vigorously scratch among the leaf litter looking for food, mainly insects. When several towhees feed in the same area, they resemble a flock of wild turkeys. Towhees build their cup-shaped nest on the ground, usually in a thicket or high grass. They lay two to six brown-spotted, cream-colored or greenish eggs. Females incubate the eggs for about thirteen days, and hatchlings leave the nest ten to twelve days after emerging. Although the nest is typically hidden, towhees are a frequent victim of the cowbird, which lays its eggs in the nest. In most cases the towhee will raise the cowbird's young along with its own.

Once past the falls, a red-marked trail makes travel faster and easier. The path continues to work its way though a deep forest. Musty odors, mushrooms and moist soils characterize the route. Downed trees lie haphazardly in the forest, occasionally blocking the way. The trail ends at a blue-marked trail and heads west (left). The route then climbs the High Peters Kill Ridge. The climb is steep and rocky, and the air becomes noticeably less humid. This 400-foot ascent is by far the most difficult part of the hike. Body heat builds quickly, and on sunny days the air temperature quickly increases as well. Tall hemlocks yield to shorter oaks and twisted gray birch. Mountain laurel becomes the dominant understory shrub.

Once completed, the ascent ends atop a high ridge with little relation to the forest below. The route levels and progress becomes easier. A forest quite unique among the Shawangunks covers the ridge top. Unlike nearby high ridges, there are few pitch pines here. Grasses, rather than blueberries, cover the ground. Big round outcrops of the Gunks' massive conglomerate beds break the surface. Some of them run in long spines in alignment with the entire range. The area's most striking features are the miniature stately oaks covering the ridge. The oaks spread their branches in wide arcs, but there remains enough space between them to allow lots of sunlight to bathe the ground.

Winds slip through the high grasses, causing them to glimmer in waves of green and gold.

A series of limited views open to the east and northeast along the open ridge. In a few spots the openings widen enough to warrant a stop. Almost straight down the cliff wall, the Peters Kill rushes though its rough and tumble valley, the sounds of the racing water rising over the cliff. Although none of the falls are visible, part of the power plant ruins are. The Peters Kill Valley looks like a canyon from this perspective. Across the canyon rises Dickie Barre, scarred with abandoned ski slopes. The Ski Minne venture ended more than twenty-five years ago as snow making and the steeper slopes of the Catskills and Adirondacks made the area obsolete. Now, natural forest processes are reclaiming the land. Farther to the northeast the ridgeline builds to Eagle Cliff and Sky Top.

After the open viewpoint the trail diverges from the cliff. The forest becomes younger—a collection of fence post-like stems. More pine works its way into the forest. The land remains flat as the path winds its way back to the main road. Traffic sounds drift over to the trail, but the road remains hidden. In a long bout of anticipation, the trail winds through the forest until meeting with the road and the parking area.

Situated along the western Gunks' western flank, this area, especially the High Peters Kill Ridge, receives less use than other sections. In many ways this is a blessing, as it provides an opportunity to experience the recovering forest and its wildlife with fewer disturbances from other people. Between the water-rich environments along the Peters Kill and the dry, exposed slopes atop the ridge, the hike has something that appeals to almost everyone.

# Lake Minnewaska and Beacon Hill

Lake Minnewaska

In contrast to the working hotel and preservation of a by-gone era at Lake Mohonk and the Mohonk Mountain House, Lake Minnewaska's grassy fields and recovering forest better represent the modern Shawangunks and their role in contemporary society. The area, once the site of two great Victorian hotels, Cliff House and Wildmere, is now adorned with picnic areas and parking lots. Building footprints and open slopes are reverting to field and forest, but more people than ever come to enjoy the scenery and recreation. Peppered with park facilities and modern conveniences, the lake is not completely free of its man-tamed past.

Before the grand hotels and their marketing, which changed place names to make them more intriguing, Lake Minnewaska was known as Coxing Pond. In that post-Civil War era the mountains were more wild and remote. Bobcats and even panthers stalked the remote pine and

# Hike: Lake Minnewaska and Beacon Hill

**Distance:** 3.00 miles

**Parking:** Upper lot of Minnewaska State Park Preserve, located along Route 44/55, 5.4 miles west of the intersection with the western end of NY 299 and 5.9 miles east of the intersection of route US 209 and Route 44/55.

**Fees:** $5 per car at Minnewaska State Park Preserve. Yearly pass available.

**Difficulty:** Easy

**Elevation change:** (lowest to highest points on route): 260 feet

**GPS reference points:**

| | |
|---|---|
| Parking area: | 41°43.102' N, 74°14.699' W |
| Beacon Hill: | 41°44.108' N, 74°13.616' W |

**Details:**

0.00 Begin from upper parking area. Take red-marked Lake Shore Drive Carriageway to the right (west). Keep the lake to the left.

0.95 Cross dam at lower end of Lake Minnewaska. After dam leave trail and follow shore line or follow Lake Shore Drive uphill.

1.15 Informal shore trail rejoins Lake Shore Drive. Continue uphill to Cliff House site.

1.30 Cliff House site. Cut across open area to lower set of picnic tables.

1.40 Yellow-marked Beacon Hill trail leaves from northeast corner of picnic area.

2.25 Beacon Hill 1,520 feet. Leave via orange-marked Beacon Hill Carriageway.

2.80 Carriageway ends at park's main road. Turn left and follow the road uphill to return to parking area.

3.00 Upper parking area. End of hike.

oak forests. Few roads penetrated this wilderness, and without any useful land for agriculture or grazing, there was little need to come to the mountains. Today, much of the area is coming full circle and regaining more of this wild character. Golf courses and apple orchards are being reclaimed as open meadows and young forests. Deer, wild turkey, bobcats, and even the occasional black bear now roam these woods.

Many trails, mostly old carriageways constructed to allow guests access to the Shawangunks' splendor, converge around Lake Minnewaska. As a result, exploring the area is often confusing. A red-marked carriageway, Lake Shore Drive, encircles the lake and junctions most of the trails heading into the park preserve. With so many route choices and so many scenic spots, most of the routes are worth exploring, but a few paths stand out when it comes to accessing the area's charm and beauty. For this hike, travel counterclockwise around the lake. Following the red-marked carriageway around the lake makes a for a nice hike, but when combined with the foot trail to Beacon Hill, it then includes a walk through a pitch pine forest and a great view of the northern Gunks' sawtooth ridgelines and the eastern Catskills' high, rounded mounds.

From the parking area at the elongated lake's north side, the site of the Wildmere Hotel from 1887 until 1986, the red-marked carriageway skirts the water's short northern edge before dropping to the shoreline along the water's northwestern corner. The Wildmere was part of the Lake Minnewaska resort run by Alfred H. Smiley, part of the same family that still owns and operates the Mohonk House. Although not as upper-class oriented as the Mohonk House and less restrictive socially, only an upscale "Christian" clientele called on the resort's graceful Victorian structures.

Massive conglomerate cliffs outline much of the lake basin. The rock platform along the lake's northern edge was the Wildmere's front lawn and provided a magnificent overlook. Higher cliffs stand along the lake's eastern shore, while steep slopes covered with a dense forest of hemlock, maple, oak and white pine lift along the slightly less rugged western shore. A few of the white pines soar above the dense,

Maps created from TOPO!© National Geographic (www.nationalgeographic.com/topo)

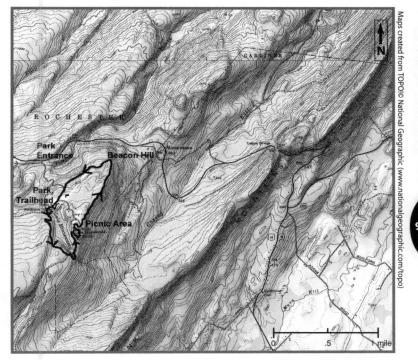

green forest canopy, their flexible trunks allowing them to gather light without competition, yet giving the tree the ability to weather high winds and ice. These tall, flexible trees were considered one of the American colonies' most valuable exports for Great Britain and her formidable navy, as many white pine trunks became ship masts.

Once down the hill from the Wildmere, the trail intersects with a few other informal trails and two other carriageways as it reaches the lakeshore and widens into a boat launch and major junction with the green-marked Awosting Carriageway. The launch provides a pleasant view across the lake to the high, stark cliffs along the lake's eastern side. With a little imagination, a ghostly outline of the Cliff House seems to shimmer above the cliffs.

After almost touching the water, the trail bends sharply left and climbs the steep, forested slopes ringing the western lakeshore. Evergreens abound—hemlock and mountain laurel are common. Once above the lake, the forest sports more sassafras. Sassafras is easy to identify because most of its leaves have three large rounded lobes. Crushing almost any part of the plant releases the aromatic scents that make sassafras tea a long-time favorite. Sassafras are genetically ancient trees, with fossil leaves found throughout the world. Pitch pine and gray birch also join the forest, lending white highlights and evergreen needles to the landscape.

The carriageway continues to head uphill at a gentle pace. Through the trees, tiny sparkles from the lake dance through the collage of branches, leaves and needles. An orange-marked trail heads west (right) through an old orchard. Lake Shore Drive then passes an overlook peering across the lake at white cliffs and a contemporary private residence.

Working its way above the shore, the carriageway arrives at another overlook with a view across the lake. The Devil's Path, part of the Catskills, rises in the distance. The lake often takes on a deep greenish hue. White gleaming cliffs, as bright as snow in the sunshine and often

The view east from Beacon Hill includes Sky Top and the Coxing Kill Valley.

brighter than the clouds on a gray day, line the lake's eastern shore. Many broken pieces of the white, angular rock lie haphazardly at the water's edge and in the lake. Like the base of American Falls at Niagara, the huge boulders are an imposing site. Imagining the amount of energy unleashed when they fall is hard to fathom, the sound booming across the lake and reverberating through the forest.

After the overlook the trail crests and drops back to the lake. Away from the lake, the forest shows more signs of the dry conditions dominating the Gunks. Millbrook Drive joins the carriageway from the west. The trail then doubles back to reduce the rate of descent as it returns to lakeshore. The moist slopes are covered with black birch. Whenever one of these trees falls, its wintergreen fragrance fills the air. Indians and pioneers collected the wintergreen oil and boiled it down into a syrup much like maple syrup. The twigs can be used to make a wintergreen tea. Black birch is a medium-sized tree, and its wood, which darkens with age, is sometimes referred to as mountain mahogany.

Before the trail settles down along the lake, another sharp rise introduces a view to the southeast situated about 300 feet higher than the Bayards (the section of ridge to the east) and the rising layers of Millbrook Mountain to the southeast. The perch provides a nice overview of the neighboring ridge and, beyond it, the Plattekill Hills. Continuing through a series of switchbacks, the trail then snakes to the lake's south side and crosses the dam. Oaks become the dominant tree along the route, the tiger-striped bark of northern red oak mixing with the wide, thick ridges of chestnut oak.

The dam presents a good opportunity to study the lake's physical geography and geology. It is likely the lake's water level was once higher than it is today—the area of the dam itself was probably underwater. In geologic terms Lake Minnewaska is close to eroding itself out of existence. To the south, the land quickly drops into the Coxing Kill Valley. A chaotic, swampy wetland gently slopes away from the lake. If it were not for the man-made dam, the remaining conglomerates would soon erode, and as each rock layer wore away, a bit more of the lake would escape. Once the Coxing Kill's vigorous flow erodes up to the lake opening, the water level will drop to reflect the evolving terrain.

The dam also provides a look down the lake's long axis, about one-half mile of open water. Yellow-green pitch pine needles dominate the east side of the lake, while the dark green hemlock and white pine needles paint the western shore. This difference is due mainly to soil depth and sun exposure. The rocky cliffs are much less hospitable to trees than soil-holding slopes.

Once beyond the dam, a short spur trail traces the lake's south-eastern edge and provides a nice set of extra views of Lake Minnewaska. The trail ends at an old dock mooring. The return to the carriageway requires backtracking, or a rougher journey up the rocky slope using a series of well-worn, but informal and winding trails back to the red-marked carriageway. Two features stand out in this area: hemlock trees and conglomerate cliffs. Hemlocks are common between the high cliffs and the lake, their roots reaching to the lake itself. The area between the cliffs and the water provides enough water and shelter for this moisture-loving conifer to thrive. Unfortunately, this area is also prime habitat for the hemlock woolly adelgid, an insect accidentally introduced from Asia. Without effective control, this pest could kill almost every hemlock in the Gunks. A close-up examination of the cliffs reveals their massive, resistant structure. Together the cemented sand grains form one of the Appalachian's hardest rocks.

Once back on the carriageway, the trail swings right (east) and opens into two, east-facing views of the gap delivering Routes 44/55 from the Wallkill Valley. Also visible are Millbrook Mountain, the Wallkill Valley and, farther east, the Plattekill Hills. As the carriageway reaches the area once dominated by the Cliff House, a series of trails crisscrosses the area. Even the main trail splits: one section heads to the site of the Cliff House, and the other route veers right (east) toward a picnic area and the terminus of the Beacon Hill trail.

A short detour to the top of the cliff adds a great highlight. The Minnewaska Cliff House was the larger of the two Minnewaska hotels and the centerpiece of the 10,000-acre resort. Although the hotel is no longer standing, the glorious overview of the lake and the Catskills remains. To the northwest rise the central Catskills highest peaks, including 4,180-foot Slide Mountain.

On the ice-polished cliffs, tracks of the last continental ice sheet are frozen in time. The direction of the scratches is the direction the ice was flowing when it last moved over the area. (No marks are left when glaciers recede, since the ice melts in place.) In some areas the conglomerate is polished to feel and reflect like glass. To the northeast, a limited view skims along the Shawangunk ridge and leads the eye to the stone tower at Sky Top.

To continue the route, the best option is to backtrack from Cliff House and head down to the picnic area along the red-marked trail. From the picnic area, the yellow-marked Beacon Hill Trail leaves from the northeast corner. The foot trail twists and turns during its first few steps, and following the trail markers can be difficult. The route soon passes over a small stream bed and crosses its tiny valley, but the intermittent waterway is dry during most seasons. Still, the extra moisture allows moss and lichens to grow near the watercourse. Large colonies

Looking northeast from the trail near Beacon Hill

of rock tripe, an edible species, call the rough rocks home. Rust, dirty white and yellow-green are the dominant colors.

Once past the small valley, the trail enters an even drier area. Pitch pine is the dominant tree, and its dry needles carpet the ground to crunch when stepped on. To the east the land drops sharply into the Coxing Kill Valley and then rises again as the Near Trapps. The trail parallels the edge of this sharp drop. There is very little soil, and the landscape is exposed to sun, wind and ice. Along the semi-open ground a scattering of pitch pines colonize the area, but large outcrops of white conglomerate stand out like mountain bones. Farther away from the drop off, the forest grows denser and a thick collection of unkempt scrub oak, chestnut oak and gray birch marks the forest community.

The trail remains level as it winds through the rough land, but it keeps providing hints of views to the east and north that never materialize. None of the areas is inviting enough to linger. In summer this ground heats quickly and there is no water along the barren land. On the hottest, driest days, the pitch pine look as though they might burst into flames. With little shade, it is easy for a hiker to overheat or dehydrate. Like many other places in the Gunks, this environment is prone to fire, and the local plant life reflects this combustible heritage. All the dominant species—mountain laurel, pitch pine, chestnut oak and blueberries—thrive after forest fires.

Glacial erratics, boulders abandoned by the ice when the last glaciers melted, pepper the ground. Although most of the erratics came from local sources, some of the transported stones and grit dropped in the Shawangunks came from the Catskills, and even the Adirondacks! Chattermarks and glacial scouring mark the conglomerate. It was not the ice, but the rock and grit carried in the ice, that produced the markings. Much of the exposed rock is polished, more evidence of the land's past immersion in a mile-thick sea of ice.

As the ridge continues to the north and east, it reaches an abrupt corner of rock where the ridge is interrupted by the ice-gouged fault delivering Routes 44/55 through the Gunks. This spine of conglomerate, which emerges above the Wallkill Valley at Sam's Point, is at the northern end of its run. North of this position, the rock layers are less solid, rising and falling as a set of knobby knolls and a trio of formations—Dickie Barre, Ronde Barre and Rock Hill—before crumbling into the Rondout Valley.

The foot trail emerges from the southwest, marking its terminus as it joins with the orange-marked Beacon Hill Carriageway. Beacon Hill is the leading edge of the unbroken rock spine heading up from Sam's Point, and its northern terminus commands an extraordinary view. The promontory is the perfect place to set a beacon, and it was one of many used in the Revolutionary War to warn of British advances. From here the land drops sharply to the northwest, north and northeast, and a large, slanted boulder provides a front row seat of the scenery. On warm days the sun-heated rock becomes a perfect resting and picnic spot. Even on the hottest days, the northern orientation prevents Beacon Hill from reaching the temperatures attained on places elsewhere in the Gunks with a southern exposure. Pitch pine and gray birch surround the open rock, but the trees do not provide shade or shelter from the wind and sun.

Looking east, the Gunks' easternmost conglomerate backbone cleaves the view in two. North of Beacon Hill, the mountains' eastern front, the anticline upholding Millbrook Mountain and the Trapps, carries the Shawangunk standard. The diagonal of white, resistant rock and cliff faces leads the eye toward the sturdy rock tower at Sky Top. Farther east the land drops from the Gunks' cliffs into the Wallkill Valley.

As the eye heads north, it leaves the Shawangunks and delves into the wide, fertile valleys of the Rondout and Esopus creeks. These broad lowlands, all once part of the 200-mile-long glacial Lake Albany, end at the feet of the Catskills, whose peaks rise more than 3,000 feet from the valley. In the forefront of this neighboring range are Overlook Mountain (3,180 feet), Mount Tremper (2,700 feet) and High Point (3,098 feet). Often, when there is a wind from the south or east, the Catskills generate their own cloud cover as warm air from the Hudson Valley climbs their slopes and condenses the water vapor. On other days the Catskills hold storms and clouds back, keeping the

Shawangunks from facing the worst of winter's assaults as they plow in from the north and west.

The return trip to Lake Minnewaska is an easy walk along the Beacon Hill Carriageway. The route is more stroll than hike. Hard rock is replaced with shifting gravel and soft dirt. A mixed forest of hemlock, red maple, oak and birch lines the trail, the shade a welcome change from the exposed foot trail. Mountain laurel dominates the understory, its pink and white flowers brightening the forest in June. The carriageway moves through habitat with more of the resources needed by forest communities. The thicker soils, additional water and greater nutrient pools support taller and older trees, along with more wildlife. Seasonal streams cross the path, their recessed beds revealing the greater soil depth and the well-developed root mat. In the topmost branches ravens roost among the taller trees. When startled from below, these huge, black birds take off in a flurry of activity.

Chipmunks dart through the forest, their high-pitched warnings an alarm to their brethren looking for food. Scrambling chipmunks are common as they work to gather the sustenance needed to survive the winter. Between predators, starvation and disease, only one in five will survive the winter. In spring, and again in late summer, each female will have one to three young.

The orange-marked carriageway is short, barely a half-mile. The route is straight and traveling is easy. The trail ends at the preserve's main road, just below the maintenance and parking area. By following the road uphill (left), it returns to the parking lots and the north side of Lake Minnewaska. Together the loop around Lake Minnewaska and Beacon Hill provides a better hiking experience than doing either one alone. The contrast of wet and dry, lake and mountain, and sun and shade are all hallmarks of the Gunks, and this loop is one of the best ways to experience all of these while enjoying some of the range's best views.

# GERTRUDE'S NOSE

Along the cliff to Gertrude's Nose

## Hike: Gertrude's Nose

**Distance:** 6.70 miles

**Parking:** Upper lot of Minnewaska State Park Preserve, located along Route 44/55, 5.4 miles west of the intersection with the western end of NY 299 and 5.9 miles east of the intersection of route US 209 and Route 44/55.

**Fees:** $5 per car at Minnewaska State Park Preserve. Yearly pass available.

**Difficulty:** Moderate

**Elevation change:** (lowest to highest points on route): 550 feet

**GPS reference points:**

Parking area:      41°43.102' N, 74°14.699' W
Gertrude's Nose: 41°41.676' N, 74°14.910' W
Millbrook Mountain Trail junction:
                         41°45.493' N, 74°09.911' W

## Details:

0.00  Begin from upper parking area and take red-marked Lake Shore Drive Carriageway to the right (west).

0.80  Take right (southeast) on yellow-marked Millbrook Drive.

1.05  Veer left, remain on Millbrook Drive.

2.00  Leave carriageway and continue straight on red-marked Gertrude's Nose Trail.

2.50  Cross power line.

3.00  Gertrude's Nose.

3.80  Cross power line.

4.70  Reach junction with red-marked Millbrook Mountain Trail. Turn left (north).

5.10  Cross Coxing Kill.

5.85  Return to southern end of Lake Minnewaska and Lake Shore Drive. Turn right (east), but can go around lake either way.

6.15  Cliff House site.

6.70  Upper parking area. End of hike.

Gertrude's Nose is a place that is easy to find, but hard to reach. Stationed at the point of a sharp peninsula of elevation, its great vista perches atop a tapering ridge. The Nose is the southernmost extension of Millbrook Mountain and Sky Top, and is the southern terminus of the Gunks' easternmost anticline. From Ulster County Route 7, State Route 299 and New Paltz, Gertrude's Nose boldly stands like the bow of a giant ship. The exposed rock ledges invite all who love mountain views, and Gertrude's Nose does not disappoint.

Hikes leading to Gertrude's Nose require a trek over Millbrook Mountain or a walk from Lake Minnewaska. The hike to Millbrook Mountain repeats much of the terrain and makes the additional hike to Gertrude's Nose seem repetitive. In contrast the route from the state preserve is more diverse, full of additional views and provides a better perspective of the Nose's rock structure and setting. Much of the route traces the eastern edge of the steep and isolated Palmaghatt Ravine, one of the lush, glacially enhanced valleys characterizing the Gunks. Other advantages of the Lake Minnewaska approach are the option of a loop, and a visit to some additional views from the upper Coxing Kill Valley.

From Lake Minnewaska's southeast corner (see Lake Minnewaska-Beacon Hill hike), the route to Gertrude's Nose follows the yellow-marked Millbrook Mountain Drive. Sharing the route with the Hamilton Point Carriageway for a short distance, the trail quickly moves from the moist habitats surrounding the lake to a drier forest dominated by gray birch, chestnut oak and pitch pine. Mountain laurel, huckleberries and blueberries grow so thick that they completely hide the ground. Like so many places in the Gunks, this forest ecology is dominated by fire, and the species growing here benefit from, or even require, flames to reproduce successfully.

Another major factor in determining the Gunks' forest composition is the infertile chemical components of Shawangunk conglomerate. Unlike softer rocks in the nearby valleys, the conglomerate breaks down slowly and the sandy soil it produces provides few nutrients for plant growth. Since sands do not hold much water, the soil dries quickly, favoring plants able to withstand semi-arid conditions despite the forty to fifty inches of annual precipitation the mountains receive. The dry, excessively drained and shallow soils are a major factor in the region's propensity to burn.

The trail soon forks left from the Hamilton Point Carriageway, maintaining its yellow markings as it bends to a more southerly course. A young forest escorts the trail. Few of the trees are more than eight inches in diameter or more than forty feet tall. With fire a constant element in the system, and its impact enhanced through the additional, intentional fires set by the huckleberry pickers until the 1960s, the forest has had little chance to mature. First generation trees, many the coppiced descendants of previous stands, dominate the slopes.

Fires were prevalent in the Shawangunks until the 1950s. Since then, fire suppression has had the upper hand and been the dominant management tool employed. Even though events such as the 1988 fire in Yellowstone National Park and the 1999 fire near Los Alamos, New Mexico, have focused attention on the role and necessity of fire, the Gunks' proximity to people and property makes it difficult to undertake controlled burns. Where fire suppression is successful, the fire-dependent species diminish and the organic material that fuels even larger fires increases. Fire suppression changes forest composition. In the Gunks, this favors gray birch and red maple over pitch pine and chestnut oak.

The longer fires are suppressed, the more severe the eventual burn will be. Severe burns are harder to control and cause more damage to the forest. Trees that survive light burns will die after hotter fires. Dead trees cannot hold soil, allowing erosion to remove the area's limited nutrient and support pool, making recovery even more difficult. Hotter fires are also more likely to rage out of control and cause property damage and threaten human life. While fire suppression may prevent some fires in the short term, it is not a question of if, but when, a Shawangunk wild fire will burn out of control.

Soon the trail lifts above the steep cliffs hemming Palmaghatt Ravine and follows the sheer line of rock all the way to Gertrude's Nose. The strong ledge and sheer cliffs are part of an anticline broken by an ancient fault. The weak rocks along the fault provided a path of less resistance to draining water. Over time, this weakness set the

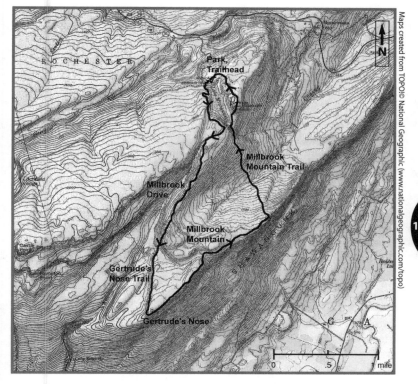

Maps created from TOPO!© National Geographic (www.nationalgeographic.com/topo)

ravine's location. Glaciers further widened the valley. The ravine's sheltered headwaters are ideal hemlock habitat, whose dark foliage dominates much of the cooler, east-facing slopes. In contrast, more fire-tolerant species line the area around the carriageway.

Situated along the anticline's gentle up-trending curve, corresponding rock layers are slightly higher where they line the ravine's western edge. It is easy to visually align the layers on each side of the ravine. Before water, wind and ice ravaged the valley, this area was all part of a gentle high slope similar in topography to the land east of the carriageway. Like a mirror image, the white walls across the ravine hold the Hamilton Point and Castle Point carriageways (the latter following the wall's top edge) in a position comparable to Millbrook Mountain Road.

The next major landmark appears where a large misplaced boulder greets the trail. Patterson's Pellet is among the trail's more impressive curiosities and viewpoints. A glacial erratic, the Pellet is a conglomerate boulder transported by the ice sheet and dropped when the ice melted. The Pellet is one of many thousands of glacial erratics scattered throughout the Gunks. Some of these mismatched rocks have sources that are much farther away; erratics originating from the Catskills, and even the Adirondacks, can be found in the Shawangunks. As with most of the land shaped by Shawangunk conglomerate, Patterson's Pellet is rough and angular. Despite all the glacial polishing and erratic boulders abandoned by the Wisconsin ice sheet, the resistant conglomerate kept erosion to a minimum, especially compared to other mountainous areas.

The view from Patterson's Pellet overlooks the expanse of Palmaghatt Ravine, the eye free to dive into its depths and climb up the other side. Broken conglomerate—jumbled into a huge talus slope— still angular and sharp, peppers the cliffs' bases. Beyond the ravine, the land rises again. Steep slopes covered in oak, red maple and birch give way to bone-white cliff faces capped with a thin, dark layer of pitch pine. On the plateaus the vegetation is a mix of green and white, the sun-baked, exposed habitat harsh and unforgiving.

The extensive view of the cliffs continues to highlight Hamilton and Castle points. Smaller ridges then lead the eye all the way to New Jersey. The view takes in 1,803-foot High Point, New Jersey's highest point, and continues down the Kittatinny Ridge, a direct extension of the Shawangunks. In the mouth of Palmaghatt Ravine, emergent white pine trees burst through the forest canopy. Their exposed crowns are all well-flagged, telling of winter winds that flow down the ravine and into the valley.

After Patterson's Pellet the carriageway slowly moves higher as it extends onto the peninsula tipped by Gertrude's Nose. Open rock ledges regularly provide views of the ravine, but none are as extensive as Patterson's Pellet. One view does open to the southeast revealing West Point and Breakneck mountains, and provides a distinct contrast between the Gunks' high ridges and the Hudson Valley's softer contours and colors. Gnarled pitch pine and chestnut oak continue to dominate the forest, although the toothed, triangular leaves of gray birch are also common.

The route changes dramatically as the Millbrook Mountain Drive veers east and a red-marked foot trail heads for Gertrude's Nose. Immediately the trail moves onto the cliffs escorting the ridge and presents a series of open views. All are similar—Sam's Point and the Palmaghatt Ravine, the high ridge holding Minnewaska State Park Preserve—but the tree and rock-inspired frames give each view unique character. Even when the marked trail moves inland, the eye remains drawn to the curving cliffs.

The neighboring ridge to the west rises 200 feet higher than the one holding the trail. As the trail (and its informal, parallel cousins) progresses, it follows the cliffs' curving contours. Dwarf pitch pines, products of past fires and poor soil, stud the exposed cliff tops. To live, the spiky yellow-green needles defy the elements and time. With little competition from other plants, the odd-shaped trees battle Mother Nature for the right to survive. In contrast, trees in the ravine grow taller and fuller. Along the Palmaghatt Kill hemlocks line the cool, moist stream course, adding to the valley's diversity.

From these cliffs, the highest set at 1,800 feet, it becomes apparent that the land is heading for an isolated point. A triangular-shaped, 1,600-foot plateau lies before the trail. Lichen colonies are among the few forms of life that can survive the harsh conditions. Mosses can also do well since there is little competition for light on the open rock faces.

Once past this set of open cliffs, the trail almost tumbles onto the plateau. Gashes formed by rill erosion eat into the mountain slope. The water draining off the higher lands is enough to support stands of hemlock at the bottom. Next, the trail drops into a tiny valley and passes beneath the three-tiered power line, an ugly, sun-blasted interruption. The power line is a prominent landmark, but its stark track across the mountains is an unwelcome blight on the landscape. In the nadir a small algae-filled stream marks the depression. Strings of algae float like locks of green hair. Artificially kept clear, and bathed in unfiltered sunlight, the area beneath the power lines is filled with red maple and gray birch saplings. The land is baked dry, even more so than the surrounding dry forest.

After rising from the power line crossing, the trail moves through a small section of thick pitch pine forest before emerging onto a series of cliffs. Large joints—vertical cracks—create dark fissures in the massive white rocks. A few of the protruding masses form pinnacles. The jump over to them looks easy enough, but the thought of falling more than 100 feet with only an angular deathbed of rocks for a safety mat kills such thoughts. The gaps are the product of jointing, a process that weakened the rock and produced this collage of broken slabs. In places, the land drops more than 150 feet, the ground littered with huge off-white boulders that were once part of the massive ridge. When one of these boulders breaks free of the cliff and crashes into the piles below, the sound must bellow through the ravine's conical opening. Even the ridge's current outline is only temporary; many of the cliffs are overhangs destined to fall.

Although mixed with forest, the open rock faces become more dominant as the trail pushes southward. A symphony of bold staccato rock and softer, more muted forests provides a melody for the eyes. Glacial erratics and the odd shapes of the hardy pitch pine seem spread like counter-melodies. The crescendos of rock continue to grow, and the forest interludes fade into the background as the land builds to a climax. Rock and forest, rock and forest, and rock—the wavy ridges harmonize to pull the hiker to the lifting melody of exposed conglomerate underscoring Gertrude's Nose. Nature's rhythms are sometimes hard to feel, but the trip out to the final point is a prominent example of how geology and geometry can stir people at many levels.

The natural orchestra delivers its final stanza as the path emerges onto Gertrude's Nose. The view to the south and west is suddenly doubled to include the east and northeast. All the Shawangunks' familiar points remain in view, but now there is much more to compare and contrast within the scene. Stark, dry rock and yellow-green vegetation give the area a character that would not be out of place in the high forests of the desert southwest.

The view to the south and west from this perspective was captured by painter George Inness around 1885. His painting, *The Shawangunk Mountains, New York*, allows Inness to travel through time and share his view of this place from more than 100 years in the past. Inness, who became more of an impressionist as his career progressed, shows a soft Shawangunk landscape with the steep eastern slopes leveling off onto a high plain. His dramatic sky is touched with a rosy hue at the horizon. The land has not changed, but the landscape has; farmland was much more prevalent in the Wallkill Valley of the late 1800s.

Although Gertrude's Nose is this trek's climax, the scenic show is by no means finished. The trail heads north along the escarpment's eastern edge to climb Millbrook Mountain. The landscape does not change much. Pitch pines and gray birch still dominate the forest, and mountain laurel and blueberries coat the ground. Exposed rock is everywhere. The climb is not difficult. Views of the Wallkill and Hudson valleys, Taconics, Hudson Highlands and Plattekill Hills are constant companions. The crossed runways of the old Galeville Army Airfield (now the Shawangunk Grasslands National Wildlife Refuge: see related hike), are another valley landmark. White pine soar alongside the east-facing cliff, having rooted in the more fertile areas below. Protected by the cliff wall, the tall, straight pines eclipse the open vista. Known for their ability to grow taller than their competition, even when that competition is a cliff, white pine are rarely blocked from the light. The long, flexible trunks allow white pines to withstand high winds and heavy ice. This flexibility made white pine a favorite of British and, later, American shipbuilders.

The view from Millbrook Mountain is one of the Shawangunks' best. Vistas in each cardinal direction emerge from the harsh pitch pine forest. A more detailed look at the mountaintop is available in the Millbrook Mountain section, which approaches the area from Routes 44/55. The summit is also a major trail junction. Millbrook Mountain Drive, the carriageway between Lake Minnewaska and atop Millbrook Mountain, ends at a small turnaround. A red-marked foot trail, the Coxing Kill Trail, slices through its namesake and returns to the Lake Shore Drive.

The trip through the Coxing Kill Valley is uneventful until reaching the stream. Without fanfare, the rocky, bumpy path moves through a thick covering of pine, oak, birch, and mountain laurel. Stones crunch and grind against one another like broken shards of glass. Only when the cooler, damper air from the Coxing Kill begins to influence the local environment do hemlocks appear. Graceful and calm, the thicker forest takes the edge off the harsh downhill walk.

The Coxing Kill is an oasis. Cool, clear waters bubble and giggle their way down a sandy, rocky streambed. Since the Shawangunk conglomerate is so hard and composed mainly of cemented sand, there is little silt or clay to muddy the water. The laurel and other species so common on the ridges are not completely banished, but the local forest of red maple, northern red oak and hemlock is much taller and fuller than the surrounding area.

Once beyond the Coxing Kill the land reverts to a harsher nature. Rockier slopes begin to predominate and the forest opens, building to a great view to the north and west. Eagle Cliff and Sky Top, the Coxing Kill Valley, and Millbrook Mountain fill the vista. Seeing the land fall and rise so sharply underscores the Gunks' difficult and spectacular terrain. After the viewpoints the trail continues to climb, becoming steep as it parallels the stream valley draining Lake Minnewaska. The small watercourse rushes through a steep drop, and the sound of rushing water reveals the stream as more of a long cascade. Much of the water flows between and beneath the huge conglomerate boulders lining the stream course.

Soon the trail levels off and moves through a swampy area below Lake Minnewaska's southeastern edge. Grasses and an uneven topography make for uneasy, often soggy footing. Almost without warning, the rough trail emerges onto the dam and the well-manicured carriageway surrounding the lake. The carriageway in either direction returns to the parking area and completes the day's adventure (see the Lake Minnewaska section for more information).

In the spirit of the great medieval castles, Gertrude's Nose commands the surrounding terrain and provides a place of rest in a busy and sometimes hostile world. Gertrude's Nose is difficult to reach, but the quest is well worth the time and effort.

# HAMILTON POINT AND CASTLE POINT

With the exception of a short, rugged section of the Long Path, the hike to Hamilton Point and Castle Point follows the area's old, well-maintained carriage roads. The wide, shale-covered paths make the walking surface smooth, but the distance alone keeps the route challenging while providing access to some of the Shawangunks' extraordinary contrasts and scenery. From the moist, hemlock-filled forests along Lake Minnewaska to the dry, rocky and exposed cliffs upholding Hamilton and Castle points, the carriage roads along the ridgeline trace pathways full of changing environments and great scenery.

The hike begins at the former site of the Wildmere Hotel, now a parking lot above Lake Minnewaska's northern shores. The route heads west (keep the lake to the left) along the old carriage road, the red-marked Lake Shore Drive. The half-mile-long lake nestles in a bed of

The view from Hamilton Point stretching up the cliffs of Castle Point

## Hike: Hamilton and Castle Points

**Distance:** 7.60 miles

**Parking:** Upper lot of Minnewaska State Park Preserve, located along Route 44/55, 5.4 miles west of the intersection with the western end of NY 299 and 5.9 miles east of the intersection of route US 209 and Route 44/55.

**Fees:** $5 per car at Minnewaska State Park Preserve. Yearly pass available.

**Difficulty:** Moderate-Difficult

**Elevation change:** (lowest to highest points on route): 580 feet

**GPS reference points:**

| | |
|---|---|
| Parking area: | 41°43.102' N, 74°14.699' W |
| Hamilton Point: | 41°41.992' N, 74°16.255' W |
| Castle Point: | 41°42.205' N, 74°16.433' W |

**Details:**

0.00 Begin from upper parking area and take red-marked Lake Shore Drive Carriageway to the right (west).

0.80 Take right (southeast) on yellow-marked Millbrook Drive.

1.05 Veer right onto yellow-marked Hamilton Point Carriageway.

2.25 Cross power line.

3.40 Hamilton Point.

3.70 Turn right (northwest) on Long Path.

3.80 Castle Point. Continue on Long Path (to the left)

5.15 Junction with green-marked Awosting Carriageway. Turn right (east).

7.50 Reach northwest corner of Lake Minnewaska. Turn left (east) on Lake Shore Drive.

7.60 Upper parking area. End of hike.

Shawangunk conglomerate, with gleaming white cliffs looming above the lake's eastern shore. A great Victorian hotel, Cliff House, stood atop this conglomerate wall until 1978. In its prime in the late 1800s, this resort competed with the Mohonk Mountain House and the Catskills' great hotels for the most wealthy and sophisticated resort guests. Now, only a more modest, privately owned, contemporary dwelling overlooks the lake, with the rest of the area accessible to the public.

The carriage road runs down to the lake, a cool touch often gliding off the cold, green waters. Heading south, the path moves through a forest thick with hemlock, black birch, chestnut oak and mountain laurel. The hemlock's thick shade and the proximity to the rain-fed lake keep the area cooler and moister than the surrounding terrain, which in turn maintains the area as prime hemlock habitat. If undisturbed by fire, ice or cutting, the hemlock can monopolize this area as their dense shade will preclude most other species' seed from sprouting successfully. Despite the hemlock's dominance of these lakeside slopes, the presence of fire-adapted chestnut oak and mountain laurel suggests that fires have reached these slopes in the past and could again in the future. Left to nature's own cycles, a fire is almost inevitable, but with fire suppression being the rule in developed areas, the hemlocks have the inside track to continued dominance.

The red-marked carriageway follows the lake's western shore as it works its way toward the junction with Millbrook Mountain Drive and the Hamilton Point Carriageway. (For a more detailed look at this area, see the Lake Minnewaska–Beacon Hill section.) At the lake's southwest corner the trail lifts onto higher ground as it meets the yellow-marked Millbrook Mountain Drive, another wide, well-maintained carriageway. The route to Hamilton Point follows this path, heading southwest and uphill. Once leaving the water-enhanced slopes near the lake, the forest and landscape quickly reveal more characteristics of a drier environment. Paper birch and pitch pine become the dominant forest cover.

The sun rapidly heats and dries the soil now that it is free of the hemlock's dense shade. The direct, unfiltered sunlight paints harsher scenes, especially in the leafless seasons when there is little color in the landscape. Whereas the hemlock's needle layers absorb sound and soften light, the crisp oak and birch leaf litter rattles at even the slightest hint of a breeze or other disturbance. Juncos and other ground-dwelling birds were silent within the needle-carpeted hemlock stands, but each hop and jump they make here crackles with crispy static.

As the route to Hamilton Point continues, it again splits off to the

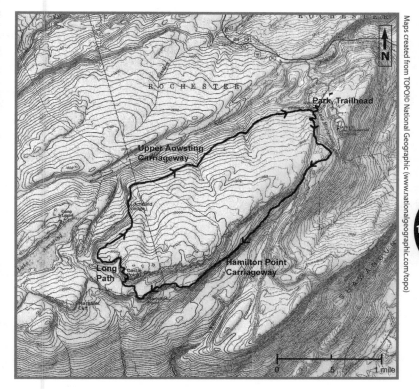

Maps created from TOPO!© National Geographic (www.nationalgeographic.com/topo)

right, shedding the Millbrook Mountain Drive (left fork) for the budding Hamilton Point Carriageway. The two routes quickly diverge, separated by the steep Palmaghatt's ravine. The junction is just above the stream's headwaters, where much of the flow seeps from the conglomerate bedrock. As the water frees itself from the rock, it becomes more readily available for plants and animals. The deep ravine, enhanced by glaciers, is enclosed by steep cliffs. Sheltered from direct sunlight, the cool slopes harbor more moisture. Water drips and slides down the rock walls, nurturing mosses and a host of small plants. With the additional moisture, forest composition changes again, with hemlock and

American beech (requiring lots of water) becoming the forest's local kings. Deep shade keeps the area relatively cool and retains moisture, keeping the habitat well-suited for the local canopy trees. Few of the fire-adjusted species so common throughout the Gunks can survive in this isolated, damp valley.

Beech bark disease is crippling many of the local beech trees. When healthy, beech bark has a smooth silvery-gray color, but many of the trunks here are blistered with ugly black scars. The infection, caused by more than one organism, begins when an insect, the beech scale, feeds on the beech trees. By themselves, these small, white insects cause little damage; however, to prevent the tree from plugging up the feeding site, the beech scale secretes a chemical into the injured bark. One side-effect of this chemical prevents the beech tree from identifying a common fungus, nectria. As a result, this aggressive fungus grows on the tree unchecked. By the time the tree can detect the fungus, which grows outward from the infection site, nectria is well on its way to encircling the trunk. If the fungus completes this ring, a process called "girdling," the tree will die. In most cases the tree can contain the fungus, but the structural damage caused by the fungus leads to rot, and the weakened tree will snap in a strong wind or ice buildup. Still struggling to survive, future generations of beech trees in these diseased areas often grow into sickly forms, their trunks heavily deformed by the disease. After about thirty years, these pitiful, disfigured specimens also collapse.

The Hamilton Point Carriageway traces the ravine's western edge, and as it continues to head southwest, the ravine's far side continues its divergent path. The ravine's southern exposure allows for temperatures to rise and warm air currents to wash up the valley. No longer tightly enclosed by the surrounding rock, the shaded glen gives way again to sun-baked slopes. Scoured white conglomerate outcrops poke through the thin covering of soil and vegetation. A look over the cliff edge reveals the ravine floor where hemlocks, beech and maples continue their dominance, but along the trail, mountain laurel and oak replace the beech and maple. A few hemlock remain. The cool, quiet environment quickly gradates into a dry, crispy forest. Rocky ledges begin to

Looking west into the Catskills from the Long Path above Castle Point

appear along the trail, the vegetation no longer able to colonize the exposed slopes. Hints of a view across the ravine tease the eye, but there are few openings worth even a pause.

Small streams cross the trail at regular intervals as escaping waters topple into Palmaghatt Ravine. The water bounces over the uneven landscape, filling the air with rhythmic song. Hemlocks line many of the watercourses, taking advantage of the cooler, wetter microenvironments. Bird life is plentiful in this mixed forest, the ovenbird's "teach-er" call a common counterpoint to the steady waters. The warm slopes also provide excellent habitat for snakes. Garter snakes are among the most plentiful species in the area, their yellow racing stripes an easy-to-identify marker. Although rare, rattlesnakes and copperheads occasionally use these slopes to sun themselves and look for prey.

While the land continues to display characteristics of a dry forest, the gradation is not complete during the first half-mile after the trail junction with Millbrook Mountain Drive. A few new tree species become more conspicuous, including shagbark hickory, white pine and red maple. Shagbark hickory is easy to identify by its large, vertically curved strips of bark that pull away from the main trunk. Although the trail-side forest is showing signs of drier conditions, a look up reveals pitch pine on the exposed slopes holding the Castle Point Carriageway—another level in dryness.

As the cliffs on the ravine's eastern side continue to retreat, the exposed rock ledges become more impressive. Finally, at a tight bend, Echo Rock, a spectacular viewpoint, provides a grand overlook of the ravine and into the Wallkill Valley. White cliffs of the resistant Shawangunk conglomerate line the valley's far side and lead to Gertrude's Nose. The tilt of the rock across the way is a cross section of the massive beds of sandy sediments laid down 420 million years ago. The rocks were last folded and raised during the Alleghenian mountain-building event, 290 million years ago. At the time, these rocks were buried under thousands of feet of other sediments that have long since eroded. The repeating wavy pattern in the cliff's edge is a result of the folding.

The cliffs provide safe nesting sites for many large birds, including peregrine falcons and ravens. Except for vultures, ravens are the most likely birds to be seen soaring above the Gunks. Still relatively rare in the eastern United States, the large black birds' distinctive "kruk-kruk" call is a symbol of the recovering wilderness. Ravens are intelligent and crafty; they can outwit prey and find hidden resources. They sail effortlessly on the Shawangunks' high quality, rising air currents, gliding on nature's free lift. The mixing of cool and warm air stirs the atmosphere and at times brings the soaring ravens close to Echo Point.

The forest and landscape lose much of their diversity once out of the ravine's influence. Poorer variations of the view to the east are constant companions. The forest settles into a mix of red maple, assorted oaks and the occasional evergreen. The next major landmark is an unusual sight within a park preserve and wild forests. Almost without warning, the carriageway rounds a curve and enters an area of low growth. Overhead three spans of heavy power lines slice the air. The imposing line of towers stands like dominos as it blasts over the main Shawangunk ridge, crosses the ravine and lifts over Millbrook Mountain. The interruption seems rude and tactless, sending a clear message of the mountain's subservient relationship to civilization. The Shawangunks are not imposing enough to keep development at bay, and they are not remote enough to be left alone. The power lines cut the mountains in two, crossing many of the hikes within the park preserve. In addition, the open ground surrounding the transmission wires is among the most exposed and sun-baked in the range.

Once beyond the power lines, the view to the east alters dramatically. Gertrude's Nose and Millbrook Mountain had filled much of the horizon. South of them, the scene to the north also opens to include more of the Wallkill Valley. In spring, the valley greens over about two weeks earlier than the mountains, and holds onto its fall color a week or two longer as well. Beyond the Wallkill Valley, the Plattekill Hills, Hudson Valley and Taconic Mountains fill the expanded horizon.

Continuing southwest, the old carriage road traces the western edge of Palmaghatt Ravine. Unusual for the eastern United States, the route provides almost continuous views. The ravine is wedge-shaped;

The eastern view from Castle Point includes Hamilton Point.

as the carriageway progresses, the valley below widens and deepens. In contrast, the trail remains at the same elevation. The drop into the ravine grows to 150 feet. While pitch pine and chestnut oak surround the trail, a look down the steep drop into the ravine reveals a forest of sugar maple and hemlock—a completely different community than that along the carriageway. On occasion, black bears can be spotted moving in the forest below.

The ledge holding the carriageway widens as it approaches Hamilton Point. A barren and exposed platform, this conglomerate cliff rises more than 600 feet above the neighboring valleys. At the heavily jointed and divided rocks forming Hamilton Point, the view becomes more engaging. A jumble of huge, angular boulders are strewn about the ground directly below the perch. Many of them fell as freezing and thawing expanded, cracked and broke the vertical joints scattered throughout this rock. Cooler climates remaining after the retreat of the last ice sheet accelerated this process. As the average temperatures warmed, this erosive action slowed, and the current, more moderated climate has decreased this activity. Across Palmaghatt Ravine, about a mile away as the crow flies, the perch at Gertrude's Nose is similar to that at Hamilton Point.

West of Hamilton Point, and a few hundred feet higher, looms Castle Point's white platforms. Like the back on a chair, the higher ledges provide a sense of security and comfort by providing a sturdy support. To the south the next jutting point along the ridge is Margaret Cliff, which offers a similar view.

After leaving Hamilton Point, the ridge loses its bee-line determination and enters a series of broken curves. In and out of the mountain mass, the carriageway works its way along the chaotic contours. The carriageway then encounters the Long Path, which offers a final climb up the Gunks' eastern face. The carriageway continues south until it merges with the trails tracing Lake Awosting.

The Long Path is the shortest and most challenging route to Castle Point, abandoning the carriageway's gentle slope for a more rugged attitude. After turning right (north) onto the Long Path, the trail quickly dives into thick vegetation. Low branches encroach on the trail. Unless rain has recently soaked the ground, the earth is bone dry. Twigs, needles and leaves crack and crunch with almost every step. Oaks, pitch pine and mountain laurel dominate the forest. A no-nonsense trail, the Long Path makes a short, steep climb to Castle Point. The trail suddenly moves from soil to rock, winds around a few large boulders and outcrops, and then spills out onto a set of open ledges. The highest ledge is Castle Point.

From atop this post, a far-reaching view unfolds to the south and west. Based on maps and the view from Hamilton Point, one would imagine Castle Point to have a view similar to Hamilton Point, but once atop this lofty perch, it is apparent that the trees and rock outcrops give Castle Point a different perspective. Castle Point has a nice overview of Lake Awosting as it nestles into the ridge top's tablelands. On each side of the rain-fed lake is a low ridge of Shawangunk conglomerate, but the lake rests on an exposed layer of Martinsburg shale. The rainbow-shaped conglomerate beds broke apart at the top of the arch to create the lake bed. The sharp slice of Huntington Ravine sits between Castle Point and the lake. The deep gash, which has a very narrow opening where it joins with the Peters Kill, may have once held a mountain lake of its own that broke through its rock dam and drained.

To the south rise the prominent towers west of Lake Maratanza and the Gunks' highest elevations. The highest rise tops off at 2,289 feet, about 80 feet higher than the ridge top west of Castle Point. To the west rise some of the southern and central Catskill Mountains, including 4,180-foot Slide Mountain, the Catskill's highest point. To the north and east are a few other Shawangunk highlights, including the tower at Sky Top and Gertrude's Nose.

Castle Point sits on an isolated corner of the ridge and provides many different options for making the return trip. Many of the routes are within a mile in terms of overall distance, but two options provide a more extensive and exciting look at the Shawangunks. The Castle Point Carriageway heads northeast from Castle Point and provides a series of extensive views to the east. The scenes are similar to those revealed along the Hamilton Point Carriageway, but from a higher per-

spective. Located atop the same ridge and often only a few hundred feet displaced from the Hamilton Point route, the ground is even drier and rockier than its parallel companion below the cliff. With less soil and sun-exposed slopes, the area is dominated by pitch pine and mountain laurel. Only as it approaches the head of Palmaghatt Ravine and Lake Minnewaska does the forest community become more diverse. The carriageway passes through the remnants of an old apple orchard and offers some views north to the Catskills before returning to the trail encircling Lake Minnewaska. This route is typically warmer than the other choices, making it more or less palatable depending on the season.

The other visually attractive route includes a trip across Litchfield Ledge and the Battlement, two more capital Shawangunk viewpoints. The carriageway is part of the Long Path. The crushed black shales contrast with the heavy white layers of conglomerate. After moving along the exposed terrain and experiencing its myriad of views, the route cuts back north to Lake Minnewaska along the green-marked

Hamilton Point

Awosting Lake Carriageway. This route is about a mile longer than the Castle Point Carriageway, but on a day with good visibility, the views are among the Gunks' most impressive.

Of special note along this route is the Battlement, another of the Gunks' erosion-defying conglomerate walls. A few hundred feet of bone-white rock provide the ridgeline's structure. To the south, Lake Awosting nestles in its high cradle. Farther south, the Shawangunks culminate as High Point, Sam's Point and Maratanza. To the west rise the Catskills, their additional heights lifting above the Shawangunk ridgeline and adding to the mountainous character of southeastern New York. Slide Mountain, king of the Catskills, rises well above its neighbors, its unbalanced summit a mark of distinction. During the last glacial advance, Slide Mountain's summit probably remained free of the ice sheet and stood alone as everything else within sight was buried beneath the icy white wave.

After following the Battlement's sweeping curve, the path continues along the cliff top perimeter and traces Litchfield Ledge. The serpentine trail is scenic. The area is so excessively drained and bereft of soil that it supports few species, mainly pitch pine, blueberry and mountain laurel. Once completing the scenic but barren trip across the ledge, the trail winds along a crumbling cliff wall into Huntington Ravine. This wide, sheltered cove is such a vegetative contrast with the mountaintop that entering the ravine is like falling into an oasis. Soaring beech and sugar maple trees shade the ground, and deciduous leaves, not fallen needles, cover the forest floor. From this junction the Long Path continues into the ravine and heads for Rainbow Falls. The fall is a graceful, low volume sheet of water. When water is plentiful, Rainbow Falls can make for a nice half-mile addition to the hike. The trail to the falls cuts through the lush forest of Huntington Ravine.

A turn north onto the green-marked Awosting Lake Carriageway heads back to Lake Minnewaska. The carriageway is an easy walk moving through a mixed pine-oak forest. Near the northern end of the trail, hemlock becomes more prevalent as water availability increases. A small picture window look at the Catskills opens before the carriageway ends at the red-marked Lake Shore Drive. Turning left onto the carriageway brings the trail to a short, steep hill before ending at the Wildmere Hotel site and the parking area.

Hamilton and Castle points are two of the most visible and scenic perches along the Shawangunks' eastern face. Reaching these exposed perches is among the more challenging of Shawangunk hikes, but the reward is well worth the effort. The route also provides many extra incentives along the way, with open ledges and unique natural communities adding to the overall experience.

# LAKE AWOSTING

Awosting is the largest of the Shawangunks' lakes. It is also the least accessible. From the parking lot at the western entrance of Minnewaska State Park Preserve, it is a three-mile hike to reach the shore. Seen from other points in the mountains, the lake is not overly impressive. It lies in a wide cleft between two of the Shawangunks' flat, high ridgelines, and its waters do not capture the surrounding forest and sky with the same glamor as its smaller and better known siblings farther north. Cliffs dominate only small sections of the lake, giving it a less spectacular setting among the Gunks' hard capstones; however, the lake's more natural setting and a scenic, inviting shoreline make it among the most enjoyable spots in the range.

All of the major carriageways traversing the preserve's main ridge wind their way to Lake Awosting. The most direct route and the best scenery mainly follow the Peters Kill Valley and Huntington Ravine.

Lake Awosting

**Hike: Lake Awosting**

**Distance:** 9.95 miles

**Parking:** Lower lot of Minnewaska State Park Preserve, located along Route 44/55, 5.4 miles west of the intersection with the western end of NY 299 and 5.9 miles east of the intersection of route US 209 and Route 44/55.

**Fees:** $5 per car at Minnewaska State Park Preserve. Yearly pass available.

**Difficulty:** Difficult

**Elevation change:** (lowest to highest points on route): 560 feet

**GPS reference points:**

Parking area:       41°42.102' N, 74°14.673' W

Eastern (lower) end of Lake Awosting:
            41°42.697' N, 74°16.926' W

**Details:**

0.00 Leave the parking area via the black-marked Peters Kill Carriageway. Almost immediately, turn left (southeast) on yellow-marked Mossy Glen Trail.

1.65 Mossy Glen Trail ends at blue-marked Blueberry Run Trail. Turn left (south).

1.85 Junction with green-marked Awosting Carriageway. Turn right (west).

2.10 Cross power line.

3.30 Awosting Carriageway ends at black-marked Awosting Lake Shore Road. Turn right (west). Begin loop around the lake.

4.90 Reach far end of lake.

6.60 Complete loop, continue along bottom of lake (small amount of overlap).

6.70 Peters Kill Carriageway heads right (north) from the Awosting Lake Shore Road.

7.15 After crossing Fly Brook, make left on blue-marked Jenny Lane Trail (also Long Path).

7.60 Cross power line (continued next page).

8.20  Junction with blue-marked Blueberry Run Trail. Turn right (south).

8.40  Junction with Peters Kill Carriageway. Turn left (northeast).

9.95  Return to parking area. End of hike.

The route begins from the lower parking area, which is just west of the main entrance. From the 1870s through the 1960s, a small hotel, the Laurel Inn, was located here. Catering to people who could not afford the region's more expensive establishments, the hotel was little more than basic lodging.

The parking area funnels into the Peters Kill Carriageway, but almost immediately a foot trail, the Mossy Glen Trail, branches to the left (southeast). Once off the carriageway, the surrounding forest closes in and produces an environment much different than the rock-lined, open and exposed carriageway. The forest is typical of the Shawangunks' middle slopes—a mix of hemlock, pitch pine, blueberries and oaks. Densely packed to form a thick forest, the trees are mostly young. As found throughout the Gunks, where poor and shallow soils are the rule, white outcrops peer from the ground and an occasional boulder juts into the trail. Struggling stems of American chestnut and northern red oak dominate much of the area. A solid layer of mountain laurel fills the understory, making off-trail movement almost impossible. Visible through the trees, especially in winter, the wide, high ridge supporting the park's highest elevations lifts to the east.

Activity abounds in the forest. Spring peepers, chittering chipmunks, drilling woodpeckers, bustling black-capped chickadees, jumpy American redstarts, and nervous yet curious, juncos are common sights. Of these creatures, the American redstart is the least common, yet sighting this flashy flycatcher is a genuine reward for the novice bird watcher. The bird grows to about 4.5 inches in length. Females are dark gray and pale yellow, while males are black with bright red and orange patches on their wings and tail. Active, even for a warbler, the American redstart feeds almost exclusively on insects. They dart, hover and jump through and on the trees as they search for

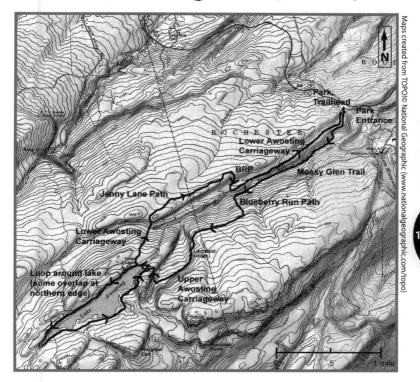

Maps created from TOPO!© National Geographic (www.nationalgeographic.com/topo)

insects. When an insect is spotted in the air, the redstart enthusiastically pursues it. Redstarts prefer second-growth habitat thick with shrubs and undergrowth—a perfect description of the Shawangunks. Nests, made mostly of grasses, bark and other plant material, are usually placed in small deciduous trees, about thirty feet off the ground.

A look through the forest reveals a large number of trees with angled trunks. Many of these belong to rings of angled trunks (coppiced trees). The angled, multiple-stem trunks give the forest a messy, irregular look. Most of the coppiced trees in this area are oaks and red maple. Appearing after logging and fires, both part of the area's history, coppiced trees grow from the surviving root systems of their predecessors to create a new set of foliage. Often more than one of these shoots survives and must compete for light with its siblings. Growing at angles away from one another helps the trees get more light, but it also weakens the limbs' integrity, making strong winds and heavy ice and snow more likely to damage or destroy the trees.

The trail parallels the carriageway as it heads southwest, with the Peters Kill running along the trail's eastern (left) side until the path descends into the tight valley and crosses the watercourse on a small bridge. The Peters Kill drains Lake Awosting and, unlike many of the Shawangunks' streams, it flows year-round. The additional moisture supports more vegetation, including large populations of mosses and lichens. Rhododendron, uncommon this far north, spreads its dark, waxy leaves and entangling limbs near the watercourse. Dallas pool, a popular swimming hole, is a little downstream of the bridge.

Once over the bridge, the trail remains along the Peters Kill's eastern side until ending a couple of miles upstream. The route is not steep, but can be challenging. Rocks and roots pave the way with uncountable small obstacles. Together, the water and rock in the stream form a pleasant percussion beat that escorts the wooded pathway. In a few places the forest yields to the sterile surfaces of Shawangunk conglomerate. Open rock outcrops, slippery when wet, spill into the Peters Kill and form its basin. At times the trail laps against the stream. The water, while free of suspended particles, has a distinctive tea color made by tannins leached from the area's many pitch pines and other conifers. Autumn brings a flood of spent leaves into the stream, creating a colorful stew made from the Gunks' forests.

Overall the trail is cooler than the sun-exposed carriageway, and there are no bikers and horses to confound the wilderness experience. In contrast with the sun-baked Peters Kill Carriageway, some sections are dominated by thick hemlock forests. In these cool, shady areas, the understory disappears. Soft needles and organic soils soak up sound. The trail crosses many intermittent streambeds. One unique feature of the Mossy Glen Trail is where it moves through tangles of rhododendron, which presents a forest much more akin to those of the southeastern United States. The Shawangunks, like the neighboring

Catskills, are a mix of species and natural communities blending elements of the northern and southern forests. Overall the Catskills are a bit more like the northern forests, while the Shawangunks are more southerly in character. The rhododendron thickets are but one example of this natural kinship.

As the trail completes its upstream migration, the surrounding land becomes a little bit drier and is more frequently interrupted by sloping conglomerate outcrops. Mountain laurel, blueberries and pitch pine blend with the oaks, maples and birches. The trail becomes a bit steeper and then dead-ends at the Blueberry Run Trail. The route continues by making a turn to the southeast (left). Without transition the trail heads directly uphill, away from the Peters Kill. It is easy to grow warm on this abrupt climb to the Gunks' widest ridge. The path is among the Gunks' steeper sections, and the low-growing pitch pine and chestnut oak forests project little shade. Black gum and aspens join the forests as well. Their respective crimson and pale gold fall foliage spruces up the area's mid-October palette. The soils become even thinner, and a population of dwarfed pitch pines struggle to survive on the rocky ground. Traction can become difficult when the trail is leaf-covered or wet. On most days the winds pick up as elevation increases. After completing the short but challenging stretch, the trail levels and then intersects the wide Lake Awosting Carriageway.

While the Blueberry Run Trail continues southeast, the route to Lake Awosting heads west (right). The green-marked carriageway is well-maintained. A chaotic forest—a scraggly collection of gray birch, oak, pitch pine and the occasional hemlock—continues to escort the path. Mountain laurel thickets hem the carriageway on each side. Although not inviting to most humans, the forest still teams with birds, small mammals, snakes and other wildlife. Level for the most part, the route is easy to follow.

A triumvirate of power lines, a major Shawangunk landmark, slices through the recovering wild forests, shattering the area's wilderness. Cutting through the forest, the power line also impacts the growing trees. The area's prevailing winds from the northwest, especially in winter, have a greater impact on the exposed trees on the southeastern side of the cut. Unprotected on their flanks and exposed to the prevailing winds, their branches and needles receive greater amounts of winter's ice and wind. This causes the exposed trees to have to spend more resources recovering from injury and replacing lost limbs. As a result they are smaller and more prone to disease. Unless a solid canopy cover returns, this trend will continue indefinitely. On the upside, the slice in the mountains does offer a limited view of the Catskills.

After passing the power line, the trail moves into the northern end of Huntington Ravine. A small perch above the sheltered valley provides a glance across the ravine to the conglomerate wall forming the valley's western limit. The carriageway winds down a short rock wall, an extension of Litchfield Ledge, as it spills into the ravine. Once below the rocky ridge top, the forest becomes more lush, taking advantage of the shelter, soil and water provided by the surrounding high lands. To the east, glimpses of Litchfield Ledge's gleaming white cliffs show through the tree cover. Pitch pine and glacial erratics stand along the stark cliffs—courageous sentinels protecting a fortress wall. Once the carriageway passes into the cooler and moister depths of Huntington Ravine, a forest of hemlock, beech, paper birch, oaks, and sugar maple come to dominate the landscape. The trees are also larger—among the Gunks' tallest. The Long Path crosses the carriageway here. To the northwest it leads to Rainbow Falls—a steep drop that is often dry, but a visual treat when water is plentiful.

After moving through the ravine, the carriageway climbs another rock wall as it exits the protected valley. Parts of the wall are eroding rapidly, the thinner sandstone layers collapsing due to exposure. The crumbling rock creates a steep, unstable slope, rather than a cliff wall. As the trail leaves the ravine, it provides one last view down Huntington Ravine and back toward Litchfield Ledge. Then the carriageway tops the divide and heads into Lake Awosting's basin. Once over the divide, hemlock becomes more frequent, often growing in dense stands.

At a three-way intersection, the carriageway merges into the loop encircling Lake Awosting. The route leads downhill over some glacially polished and scoured conglomerate. The glossy, slippery rock has the sheen of polished glass. Green glints from the lake sparkle through the oak and hemlock forest. The lake basin lies along a fault line and anticline in the Shawangunk conglomerate, the bent, broken rock less able to withstand erosion, thus forming the depression. The air feels more moist here, enhanced by evaporation from the lake. On cloudy days the lake reveals a steely-gray palette. Except in the calm of morning and evening, the water helps generate additional winds along the shore—a blessing in summer and a curse in winter.

A trip around Lake Awosting is a scenic journey, often enhanced on rainy days as cloud banks tangle with surrounding low ridges and cool water. While the lake, at 1.1 miles long, is the largest of the Gunks' sky lakes, it also has less surrounding topography than its northern brethren. Known as Long Pond before the resort owners renamed it, Lake Awosting is almost ninety feet deep. The local trails form a loop around the lake, so the journey around the perimeter can start along the eastern or western shore.

Pitch pines along Lake Awosting's western shore

The walk around the lake brings a different experience from each side. On the lake's western shore the trail remains well above the water, perched atop conglomerate cliffs. A pitch pine forest escorts the winding carriageway, in places forming a tunnel of yellow-green needles. More pines, along with mountain laurel and a few oaks, fill the ground between the ledge and the lake. From the early 1900s until the 1960s, much of this area was Camp Awosting, one of the nation's first summer camps. A few of the recreational facilities, buildings and foundations remain in place. The forests and fields are still adjusting to the area's abandonment, working to fill areas once used for recreation and picnicking.

Once at the lake's far side, the trail moves through the swampy ground holding the lake's headwaters. Although mostly rain fed, some water trickles into the basin from the surrounding bedrock. At the lake's southern end, water backs up in sluggish pools before reaching open water. At the lake's southeast corner, a spur trail continues southwest to Mud Pond, the smallest and least accessible of the Gunks' sky lakes.

The route along Lake Awosting's eastern shore remains along the water level and faithfully traces the lake's contours, cultivating intimate contact with the lake's cold, acidic waters. A look into the clear water reveals no fish, salamanders, crayfish or other aquatic life. Between the acidity in the rainwater and the lack of nutrients in the rock, the lake is hostile to most forms of aquatic life. Like many lakes in the Adirondacks, the Shawangunks' waters are little more than decorative pools among the craggy peaks and cliffs. In a few spots, short trails head out to small peninsulas. From these remote points of white rock and a few green and brown pine trees, spectacular panoramas of the lake and its western cliffs unfold. Within the water large, angular blocks of conglomerate lie strewn about the lake bed. To the east a series of spur trails head to the Shawangunks' eastern escarpment and points with intriguing names and impressive, if not repetitive, views. For hikers looking for a little extra challenge, detours to Margaret Cliff, Wolf's Jaw, Murray Hill and Spruce Glen present longer challenges.

As the trail returns to the lake's northern end, the route divorces the shore as it completes the loop. A major intersection marks the

Hamilton Point Carriageway's southern terminus. The Awosting Carriageway swings left (north) and moves into an area covered in hemlock, gray birch and oak. After moving through some rougher terrain, the carriageway completes its loop at Awosting Lake Carriage Road. Heading left (west), the carriageway slips along the lake's lower edge. The view down the lake reveals the Gunks' longest expanse of open water. Beyond the lake basin the trail quickly lifts over a divide as it begins its return to the parking area via the Peters Kill Carriageway.

At first the trail moves through a typical Shawangunk forest of oak, birch, pine and blueberry, and the trail maintains a downhill slope as it drops off the Gunks' high central ridge. A few breaks in the tree cover and rock contours provide glimpses of the surrounding Shawangunk ridges and more distant Catskills. Among the more striking areas along the carriageway is where it cuts through Fly Brook's forested wetlands. The low, wide drainage delivers water from Mud Pond, the smallest and least visited of the Shawangunks' lakes. Standing water is common in the poorly drained area, and a strong odor of rotten eggs (hydrogen sulfide) can collect when the air is still. A look up the wide valley reveals an open expanse of blueberries and huckleberries choking the ground and giving the area a reddish tint in fall and winter.

The Jenny Lane Trail, part of the Long Path, cuts left (northwest) from the Peters Kill Carriageway after crossing Fly Brook. The carriageway is the most direct route back to the parking area, but it is lacking in scenery. The Jenny Lane Trail is a much better choice. The terrain is more varied and visual delights abound. After following Fly Brook upstream, where an even wider view fills the western horizon, the path ascends a short, steep rock face and heads northeast.

In season this area could be a blueberry and huckleberry farm. In the past, the local wild berry crop in this area was harvested by a group of hearty folk known as the huckleberry pickers. They sold the sweet crop to middlemen in nearby towns. Berry picking continued into the 1960s, and the pickers often feuded with resort managers. Resort patrons considered their poor and colorful lifestyle distasteful and a detraction from their holidays. In addition the berry pickers set fires to regenerate the berry crop, and the fires often threatened property along the ridge top.

Atop the small windy ridge stands a dry forest of chestnut oak and pitch pine and a few highbush blueberries and mountain laurel. The trail is often coated by a copper-colored carpet of needles lying over hard conglomerate. The trail then passes into the wide, sun-blasted corridor created by the power lines that slice the Gunks in two. To the east it is easy to trace the power line's path across the Gunks as it cuts across the Peters Kill and Lake Awosting carriageways. To the west the slice through the mountain reveals the southern Catskills. The long straight swath devoid of trees is a strong contrast with nature's irregular lines.

As the trail continues eastward, it unveils a series of views of the 2,000-foot-high ridge to the east across the Peters Kill Valley. A few open ledges enhance this view. The trail then moves away from the small cliff and winds through the low forest until encountering the Blueberry Run Trail. The route follows the Blueberry Run Trail south along a steep downhill course into a forest of oak and laurel before cutting through a darker hemlock stand and the small, twisting stream supporting it.

The trail then emerges onto the Peters Kill Carriageway. Although not an exciting path, it is the most direct route to the parking area. After the long walk around Awosting, the easy trail can be a welcome reprieve. Compared to the Jenny Lane and Mossy Glen trails, the carriageway is like an expressway back to civilization. For those looking for a bit more adventure, the Blueberry Run Trail crosses the Peters Kill and rejoins the Mossy Glen Trail. Either route returns to the parking area.

Lake Awosting is among the less visited and more natural looking areas in the Shawangunks. Although it is a long hike by Shawangunk standards, it is well worth the trip. The mix of land, rock, water and fire-dependent forests gives the area a starkness not generally associated with the northeast.

# STONY KILL FALLS

Stony Kill Falls

**Hike: Stony Kill Falls**

**Distance:** 1.2 miles

**Parking:** End of Shaft 2A Road, off Rock Haven Road. Rock Haven Road is just off Route 44/55, 1.5 miles east of the intersection of Route 44/55 and US 209. If coming from the east, it is a right turn (not well marked) and then an immediate left. From the west, it is two left turns. Take Rock Haven Road 1.9 miles, then turn left on Shaft 2A Road.

**Fees:** None at parking area. The falls are in Minnewaska State Park Preserve, which charges a fee.

**Difficulty:** Easy

**Elevation change:** (lowest to highest points on route): 75 feet

**GPS reference points:**

    Parking area:    41°43.814' N, 74°17.897' W

    Eastern (lower) end of Lake Awosting:

                41°43.669' N, 74°18.075' W

**Details:**

0.00 From parking area follow the stream or informal trail (generally south and west) up the gentle grade.

0.30 Pass through cleared area.

0.60 Stony Kill Falls. Return using the same route.

1.20 Return to parking area. End of hike.

Stony Kill Falls is an easy-to-reach destination, perfect for when time is short, or for people not prepared for longer treks. Although not a difficult hike, the falls, arguably the most impressive in the Shawangunk range, are worth the trip. The falls' lacy water curtain cools the air, making it a great place to find relief from summer's heat. The eighty-seven-foot falls are the highest single plunge water takes while escaping the Gunks. The drop alone makes the falls a worthy destination, but for those needing additional adventure there are difficult and tricky routes to the top, where an unmaintained carriageway runs south to Lake Awosting. The falls, however, are more impressive from the bottom, and while the additional effort needed to reach the top is good exercise, it does little to improve the view.

No marked trail runs from the parking area at the end of Shaft 2A Road to the falls, but any freelance route along, or even in, the streambed quickly and easily leads to the waterfall. Shaft 2A Road, an access point to the tunnels bringing water from the Rondout Reservoir to New York City, ends in an old, rock-lined clearing stripped of its vegetation and natural dignity. Piles of broken glass sparkle without a hint of glamor. Beyond the parking area, but before entering the open site, the road crosses below the triple power lines bisecting the entire Shawangunk ridge. Within the site large metal bolts and fine gravel pepper the ground, providing a distinct contrast with the white cliffs jumping to build the Gunks' ridgeline. The ground is typically dry, and pitch pine stand out along the cliffs. Turkey vultures soar above the abandoned area in their never-ending search for creatures no longer able to continue the struggle to survive.

Shaft 2A Road ends along the Minnewaska State Park Preserve boundary. The falls and the area immediately downstream are within the park. Stony Kill Creek continues deeper into the park, its headwaters gathering on the high plains of the Badlands, a pitch pine-dominated plateau. Waters moving into the stream often gather quickly, as the soils cannot hold much moisture—one of the reasons pitch pines do so well in the Badlands and throughout the Gunks. During heavy rains the volume of water can increase rapidly, something to remember when exploring the falls and streambed when heavy rains are predicted.

Steep rock walls launch the Shawangunk ridge above the surrounding terrain. A large gap in the rock wall coincides with the Stony Kill's exit from the ridge. The stream moves off the ridge much like any stream heading for the lowlands—a rocky bed with the rushing water bouncing and tumbling along the vigorous stream course. Like a child that has just created a large mess and is trying to slip innocently away, Stony Kill exits the Gunks' main mass. A short trip upstream, however, reveals the extent of this steep rectangular valley. Glaciers enhanced

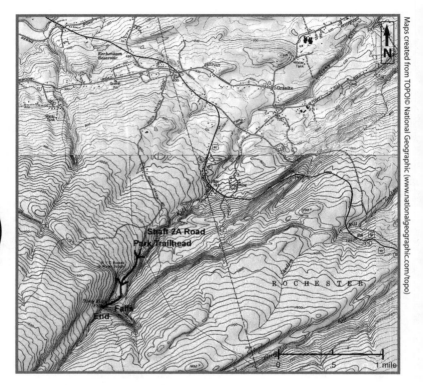

Maps created from TOPO!© National Geographic (www.nationalgeographic.com/topo)

the narrow canyon, leaving behind a hanging valley. The canyon's white walls lift 200 feet from the parking area.

At the point where the gravel road ends, it encounters the stream and a scattering of informal trails into the surrounding woods. An old concrete dam, once holding a small pool for recreation or power, bisects the waterway. Once near the cool water where the moisture blends into the nearby air, hemlocks become a major forest component. Their shady presence limits the ground cover and makes travel easier. As a result, the forest is dark, shaded and carpeted in coppery needles. Black birch is another common forest member, its strong wintergreen scent easy to detect in newly broken branches and twigs. Compared with the sun-baked terminus of Shaft 2A Road, the world is lush and green.

The streambed is full of time-worn, rounded rocks of Shawangunk conglomerate. White and gray boulders share the watercourse with smaller pebbles, a source of additional color in the streambed. Close observation reveals red and green tints among the more earthy tones. Rocks not within the streambed are much more angular. The resistant conglomerate is not easily shaped by the running water, but as the stones grind against one another, they wear more quickly. When the water is high, typically during the spring, the stream becomes a large rock tumbler.

One consistent feature of Shawangunk streams is a lack of aquatic life. The dearth of nutrients in the eroded rock, the slow rate of erosion and the predominance of acid-loving life forms such as pitch pine, mountain laurel and blueberries, make the water too acidic to support the fish, salamanders, crayfish and aquatic insects common throughout eastern North America. Although the stream environment is harsh, it is the result of natural process, and should not be confused with pollution.

After a major bend to the south, the stream opens into a natural amphitheater. A wide boulder field interrupts the streambed and demands a short climb before reaching the falls. Once at the top of the boulder field, Stony Kill Falls drops without any further ado. By any assessment the eighty-seven-foot drop and additional cascades are impressive. Before ending the lacy, single drop, the fall metamorphoses into a series of complicated jumps and bumps, adding additional depth to the plume. The water colors the underlying rock a deep brown, another contrast with the conglomerate's bleached appearance. Cliff walls flair from the fall's center.

Many horizontal layers, each a river or beach deposit from an ancient shoreline more than 400 million years ago, compose the wall. The streambed and falls cut into the resistant conglomerate beds. The lighter surroundings contrast with the shaded forest lining the watercourse, while the sound of plummeting water races down the valley.

The area's shallow soils and steep, exposed slopes make it difficult for trees to remain intact, but there is a healthy growth of hay-scented

Top of the falls

fern. Their sweet aroma permeates the area and softens the otherwise harsh look of the bare rock below. A few blackberries and some small, struggling black birch also grow along the edges. Rocks, not trees, define this landscape. Large branches and even entire trees are entangled with the rocks and boulders at the fall's base. The bleached wood and dark trunks add color and texture.

Animal life thrives among the area's rocks and ledges. Wrens and woodpeckers dart among the rocks and trees, while chipmunk chatter also fills the air. With the large number of sunbaked rocks, it is not a surprise to encounter a snake here. Among the more common snakes in the area is the black snake, also called the black rat snake. It is the largest snake found in New York State and can grow to eight feet. The preferred habitat is primarily along cliffs and rocky slopes— well-represented around Stony Kill Falls. Not a threat to people, black snakes eat birds and small mammals. They use constriction to subdue their food. Among their prey are copperheads, one of the area's poisonous snakes.

The fall's lacy nature keeps the water velocity down, and it is possible to approach the plunge without being overpowered by pounding water. The large variety of rocks and perches surrounding the falls provides many different perspectives. The wide amphitheater and lack of trees makes the falls quite photogenic. When the sun hits the water plume, the scene explodes in rainbows. Whether visited as an easy-to-reach retreat or a family day in the outdoors, Stony Kill Falls presents a great opportunity to get to know the Shawangunks a little bit better.

Starflower

# VERKEERDER KILL FALLS AND HIGH POINT

**Hike: Verkeerder Kill Falls and High Point**
**Distance:** 8.90 miles
**Parking:** Sam's Point parking area is east of Cragsmoor at the
end of Sam's Point Road. There are a few options for get-
ting into the area, all using NY 52.
**Fees:** Cars $5.00. Yearly pass available.
**Difficulty:** Difficult
**Elevation change:** (lowest to highest points on route): 500
feet
**GPS reference points:**
Parking area:      41°40.211' N, 74°21.654' W
Verkeerder Falls: 41°41.115' N, 74°19.671' W
High Point:        41°42.229' N, 74°20.671' W
**Details:**
0.00 Take left fork of paved road on leaving parking area.
0.65 Sam's Point.
1.25 Leave paved road. Turn right (southeast) on dirt road.
1.30 Turn left (east) on blue-marked Verkeerder Kill Falls Trail.
3.05 Verkeerder Kill Falls.
3.25 Turn left (north) on red-marked High Point Trail (can be
hard to follow at times).
5.65 High Point, elevation 2,246 feet.
6.00 Old fire tower site. Head left (downhill) to High Point
Carriageway.
6.10 High Point Carriageway. Turn left (southwest).
7.75 Rejoin paved loop road encircling Lake Maratanza. Turn
right (west).
8.90 Return to parking area. End of hike.

Among the region's most spectacular landscapes are those south of the Minnewaska State Park Preserve along Sam's Point Dwarf Pine Ridge Preserve's northern edge. As the Gunks reach their widest point within these areas, the land becomes accessible only by foot. It requires greater effort to reach this steep, inhospitable and striking terrain, but the experience is well worth the effort. The loop hike out to Verkeerder Falls, across the Badlands, up to High Point, and then back to Lake Maratanza and the Sam's Point Preserve parking area, is about nine miles and is one of the range's more challenging and rewarding hiking routes.

From the Sam's Point parking area, the trail begins as a decaying road. The route first follows the eastern (right-hand) branch of the paved loop road. In the past this road offered tourists a chance to drive around Lake Maratanza and visit the now defunct Ice Caves Mountain tourist attraction. The road heads north toward the massive conglomerate beds holding Sam's Point. The cliffs form an imposing wall, and it is easy to understand why the road follows this less aggressive course.

The thick white layers of conglomerate upholding Sam's Point are the crest of an anticline. Although not always easy to detect, the Gunks' sedimentary foundation is not level. On average the entire mountain range is tipped twenty-two-degrees from horizontal, with the rock layers dipping to the north and west. During the last two mountain-building events, the Acadian and the Alleghenian orogenies, these rocks were bent, warped and uplifted as continents collided. Only their distance from the impact zones kept the rock layers relatively intact. To the west, the Catskills' rock layers remained almost completely horizontal. To the east, the Hudson Highlands show deformities so great that much of the rocks' original character has been remolded.

At Sam's Point and areas directly north, the Shawangunks attain their highest elevations as the hard conglomerates crest in both height above sea level and in the bow of the rock layers. The rock layers, if traced in a southeast to northwest line, would appear much like a series of rainbows (the crests) and gutters (the stream valleys). At the top of the rainbows the rocks have been stretched, resulting in joints and other large cracks. Forming ice widens these cracks, leading to the

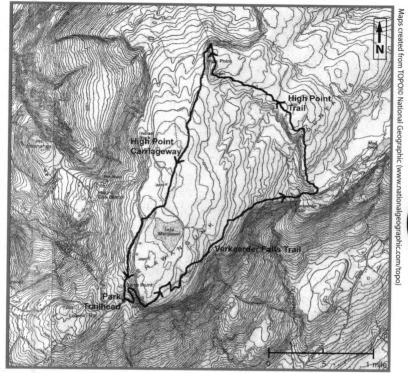

Maps created from TOPO!© National Geographic (www.nationalgeographic.com/topo)

huge talus piles found below many of the Gunks' cliffs. In the bottom of the gutters, rushing streams cut into the rock, forming small V-shaped valleys.

Along the roadside grows, by Shawangunk standards, a robust and relatively diverse forest. Capitalizing on the area's deeper soils, a more diverse assortment of trees reach for the sky. Additional nutrients also enhance growth rates. A few unlucky saplings struggle to survive among the broken pavement. Although this generation of young trees will most likely fail in its bid to colonize the regressing road surface, it is paving the way for reforestation on this barren ground.

In June, the thick clusters of mountain laurel explode in pink and white. Each blossom is a tiny show. Mountain laurel is typically associated with dry sites and fire-prone areas. Note the waxy coating on the flowers. The wax prevents the flowers from drying out, allowing the laurel to conserve water. Species that do not have means of conserving water would wilt and die more quickly on these poorly drained, sandy soils. Less hardy plants that tried to become established here withered and died long ago.

Witch hazel, chestnut, northern red oak, red maple, black birch and sassafras dominate the vegetation. As the trees grow, their shade alters the forest's microenvironments. Temperatures at ground level are cooler and soils can retain more moisture. In turn, these more hospitable conditions promote greater diversity. This process of one natural community altering an environment so that other communities can come to dominate a landscape is called succession. Some areas, like the Shawangunks' ridges, do not have enough soil to allow succession to progress beyond the current scrub oak and pitch pine forest. In other areas, like along the road, the forest may include as many as fifty tree species.

A series of switchbacks keeps the grade moderate as the route climbs Sam's Point. Between the open areas created by the roadway and the shallow soils, tree height drops and the forest appears poorly groomed. Gray birch joins the tree cover, the small, white tree becoming a major part of the local flora. In many of the open patches, sweet-smelling hay-scented ferns cover the ground. Their soft, yellow-green fronds thrive in the direct sun, but quickly die if shaded.

The roadway works its way up to the base of Sam's Point, providing a close-up of the rough, blocky stone holding the heights. A few large boulders have broken from the cliff wall as the unrelenting forces of erosion batter the resistant rock. Large fissures, the result of this breaking down process, trace black, empty lines against the hard white rock. Large conglomerate boulders line the roadside. Small caves and wide crevices are prominent. Quartz pebbles, remnants of the ancient Taconic Mountains, are found throughout the cliff face.

The roadbed soon climbs past the steep cliff face and levels off atop the ridge. Often, the wind picks up above the sheltering rock. Exposed outcrops offer expansive views to the east and south. The Shawangunks take a beeline to the southwest, and the lowlands of the Wallkill Valley lead the eye into New Jersey's northern reaches. The crowning point in New Jersey, High Point, is also the Garden State's highest elevation (1,803 feet). To the west of this ridge are the Delaware Valley and ridges and hills of Pennsylvania. To the east, the view encompasses the bumps and lumps of the Plattekill Hills. To the southeast are the chaotic summits of the Hudson Highlands, including West Point, Storm King, Breakneck Ridge and Mount Beacon. A wide gap between Storm King and Breakneck Ridge marks the narrowest point in the lower Hudson Valley, a focus for Revolutionary War strategy. By controlling the heights the rebelling colonists could control the river and prevent British ships and forces from moving toward Albany from the south. It is this strategic point that Benedict Arnold tried to hand over to the British by treachery. If he had succeeded, it could have doomed the American Revolution.

Sam's Point is named for Samuel Gonsalus, a local hunter and scout well-ingrained into the local lore. He was known for his ability to fight the Indians and prevent massacres of the local colonists. The local Indians hated Sam and set ambushes to try to kill him. Among his greatest exploits was a close pursuit where he raced to the edge of these cliffs and jumped, landing safely among the hemlock branches below the ledge.

Sam's Point also has a westerly view. Framed by pitch pine and gray birch, the rock viewing platforms open on the southern Catskills. Thunder Hill, Red Hill, Denman Mountain, Cove Pond and the Rondout Reservoir are all in view. Directly south rises Losees Hill, easily identified by its impressive radio tower. A stone safety wall, out of place among the white cliffs and pine needles, protects some of the cliffs, but it also detracts from the area's natural beauty.

After Sam's Point, the road and scenery settle into a less exciting pattern. The road keeps the thick, low vegetation, mainly oak, birch and pine, at bay. In places, cherry and apple trees, remnants from past attempts at agriculture on the ridge top, complement the regenerating

The Gunks' conglomerate backbone at High Point

forest. The trees are often widely spaced, a testimony to the wide root systems needed to find water, nutrients and support among this trying landscape. Sweet fern, a distinctive shrub that gives off a pleasant, aromatic scent when its leaves are crushed, thrives.

The road, although still mostly intact, continues to lose its battle with nature as the relentless processes of succession and erosion break down the pavement, allowing grasses and plantains to colonize the crumbling pavement. Their roots reach through the cracks and into soil covered by asphalt for decades. The land is mainly green and gray, but a few bright splashes of color—purple heal-all, white daisy, yellow buttercups, various wild pinks, lavender clover, indigo blueberry and violet thistle—advertise to the neighborhood's pollinators and add vibrant accents.

As the promontory that holds Sam's Point retreats back to the main ridge, the road heads west, centered along the rock spine. Many of the Shawangunks' shapes reveal this type of composition—a gently sloping, somewhat symmetrical ridge top that falls off quickly to either side. The profile is similar to an upside-down U.

After a short distance a small clearing and junction open to the right. Turning into the clearing, the main trail heads downhill toward the ice caves, a worthwhile, if not over-visited attraction among the collapsing conglomerate cliffs. The trail to Verkeerder Kill Falls requires a quick left turn. The green-marked trail immediately plunges into a land blanketed in blueberry, huckleberry and pitch pine. In this odd, dwarfed forest, both the land and air are dry. In summer's heat, the place is desert-like. Much of this aridity is caused by shallow soils and impenetrable bedrock. Any water falling on these slopes immediately flows downhill; little remains for the local vegetation. Thus, almost every plant that lives on these exposed slopes is ecologically suited to deal with drought and fire.

The trail follows the ridge and quickly falls in line with the land's contours, skirting along the steep drop into the Verkeerder Valley. A bronze carpet softens the route and prevents the forest's nutrients from washing down slope. The trail settles into a northwesterly course it will follow until after crossing the falls. With the vegetation unable to block the view, a series of far-reaching vistas is a constant companion, again drawing comparisons with the American west, where desert mountains also provide uninterrupted views of the surrounding landscape. The views concentrate to the north toward Lake Awosting and the white scars of the Battlement, Castle Point, Hamilton Point, Gertrude's Nose and Millbrook Mountain. To the east the viewshed includes the Plattekill Hills and the Palmaghatt Kill, and the Shawangunk Kill and Wallkill valleys.

When viewed from farther north along the ridge, the area around Sam's Point and along this ridgeline appears generic and boring. Once on the trail, however, it is apparent that the landscape is more diverse, especially along the two small streams that interrupt the dry ridgeline. The blueberries and mountain laurel give way to grasses, oaks and birch. The water-soaked lands are much more inviting to animal life. Wetlands attract birds and other wildlife, increasing the area's diversity.

Hiking in this area without noticing the blueberries and huckleberries would be like walking though an amusement park and not noticing the roller coasters. The berries grow almost everywhere, encouraged by the acidic soils, dry conditions and open ground. A tasty treat, the berries are full of flavor. From early July until late September, they remain a trailside snack for the many creatures traversing the area.

The exposed trail and open pitch pine forest is interrupted by the first of two valleys that slice into the conglomerate wall. The first stream is the output from Lake Maratanza. Along this stream the forest adds gray birch, northern red oak and red maple, a welcome break from the oppressive and stiff pitch pine forest. Unlike the twisted and undisciplined pines, the deciduous trees grow straight and tall. Sweet smelling, hay-scented fern and lush grasses carpet the ground in a soft layer of gentle greens.

Throughout the trail glacial erratics, boulders picked up and dropped by the last glacial ice sheet, pepper the land. Much of the soil atop the ridge developed from glacial deposits and the remains of the plants that grow here. The soil, almost exclusively sand and organic matter, does not contain many nutrients, nor is it effective in holding water. As a result, only a few specialized plants can thrive on the Gunks' ridge tops. Where the trail moves through these areas, erosion has removed most of the soils to reveal a cross section of the shallow ground. Roots dominate the cross section as the local plants struggle to maintain their home and conserve the scarce nutrients.

The trail once again takes on a familiar pattern as it descends into the Verkeerder Valley. Hemlock join the forest, a sure sign of more plentiful water. The air feels more humid as well. The trail begins a short, sharp descent. Grasses appear, along with oaks, birch and maple. The trail and stream meet in a jumbled confluence. A look down the braided, meandering streambed quickly reveals the water's destiny. After only thirty feet the entire stream disappears. Only when the water is high does the sound of falls cut through the stream's playful splashes.

On the north side of the fall, a few steps back toward the stream disclose a look into the fall's chasm. The fall has made a sharp gash into the Gunks' eastern front. A view out the southwest-facing opens into New Jersey, with the obelisk atop High Point a distinct landmark. As with so many places in the Shawangunks, water is often scarce. In the summer and fall the flow over the fall slows to a trickle and is little more than a dark stain against the cliff wall. The cliff face is sheer, but in the places where even small ledges can hold vegetation, hemlock, white pine and rhododendron cling to the rocks. Wild rhododendron is at the extreme northern edge of its range, the Gunks being the most northerly mountain province to support it. The southern exposure and proximity to the Hudson Valley's mild climes provide just enough warmth to support this well-beloved flowering species. Despite the lack of water during much of the year, the fall's impressive geology and ecology make a visit worthwhile any time of the year.

Once past the fall the path moves through a mixed forest of conifers and hemlocks, the additional moisture retained by the Verkeerder's valley adding to the diversity of plant life. The path leaves the valley as it climbs a rocky incline. The route is steep and more difficult than most stretches of trail in the Gunks. To the south rise the towers lining the western shore of Lake Maratanza. A natural landmark in this southerly view is the distinct forest regime defined by the Shawangunks' ridge top. The darker green, fuller deciduous trees grow in the valleys and partway up the steep slopes. As the land levels out atop the Gunks, the forest takes on more of a yellow-green hue and is shorter. This is the same forest dominated by pitch pine, blueberries and mountain laurel that the trail crossed through earlier.

Once out of the valley and atop the ridge again, the green trail ends at a red-marked trail. The trail now heads through the Badlands, a collection of pitch pine, gray birch, scrub oak, mountain laurel and huckleberries, that easily lives up to its billing. This tableland is part of the Gunks' highest platform, culminating near High Point, which is visible as a small promontory to the northwest. Moving along the northern side of the upper Verkeerder Valley, many open views, all variations on the same theme, escort the trail. The most impressive view includes the Catskills in the northwest and the Hudson Highlands to the southeast.

White boulders, glacial erratics, lie haphazardly strewn over the ground. An uneasy collage of mountain, rock, tree and root, the path is distinctive, but disturbing. Adding to the chaos is the myriad of twists and turns the trail uses to confuse hikers. Small ledges, protruding outcrops and thick brush add additional obstacles. Although moving through the area often includes losing the trail, the valley's constant companionship and parallel course allows for leaving the trail and returning without much fear of becoming disoriented. To the northwest the low rise marking High Point creeps ever closer.

Much of the exposed rock has been glacially polished. The hard conglomerate takes on a glassy sheen. It is even slippery when crossed, especially when wet. The streaks reveal the direction the glacier was moving when the ice and its rocky cargo skidded and scratched its way across the Shawangunks. The hard, impervious rock does not hold water and shunts it down slope where it becomes surface runoff. Rainstorms in the Badlands quickly overwhelm the dry rivulets. The result of this excessive drainage is that despite the forty-five inches of annual precipitation this area receives, the ground does not hold much water. The lack of available moisture influences the local vegetation. Most plants dominating this landscape—pitch pine, blueberry and mountain laurel—are typically associated with dry landscapes.

The trail continues its westward march toward High Point, and the ridge upholding it appears a little more impressive as it begins to dominate the landscape. The Verkeerder's headwater valley blends into the plateau-like Badlands. The trail becomes easier to follow as it moves into a less rocky area. A wide, unmarked route branches off to the left (south) and heads for a large clearing where it joins High Point Carriageway, but this shortcut bypasses High Point's extraordinary vistas. After a short climb over rocky ground, the trail emerges atop the rock spine holding High Point.

High Point is among the Gunks' loftiest crests, topping off at 2,246 feet, just a few feet shy of the Gunks' highest elevations. Atop the exposed rock lies a government survey marker, which is noted on U.S. government topographical maps. From the exposed platform another extensive view opens, featuring a fine look along the Gunks' spine as it heads northeast. In the west, the Catskills fill the viewshed. Most prominent among the soft, rounded peaks are Red Hill and Thunder

Hill. To the southeast rise the Hudson Highlands with their bumpy, chaotic forms.

Across the gentle bow of the Gunks' ridge top is a curious scene presenting a pitch pine-studded landscape. The blend of shrub and pine creates a distinct texture over the mountaintop. In many ways the scene resembles the Joshua tree forests of the southwest. As the rock ridge moves to the north, views of the Catskills, Berkshires and Taconics open. The Ashokan Reservoir and Ashokan High Point are the most prominent sites.

Continuing north along the ridgeline, the trail moves through a series of boulders and outcrops until reaching the northwest edge of High Point. A lookout tower, built around 1920 and removed six decades later, once stood at the site, its mounting hardware still visible. The area is a scraggly mix of broken rock, slipping slopes and struggling vegetation. Like the lost lookout tower, this viewpoint's best days were in the past. Overall the steep drop to the west and north provides another set of views similar to those atop High Point. The only addition is the white cliffs of Napanoch Point, another promontory on the Shawangunk ridge.

A wide, rocky trail heads south, quickly merging with the High Point Carriageway. From this point the route is easy to traverse and almost painfully flat. In season the large stocks of blueberries and huckleberries provide enjoyment. The trail is not nearly as well-preserved as the carriageways to the north. Wide and open, the surface is packed with dirt, rather than covered with crushed shale.

Although the vegetation is taller and more diverse than along the Badlands, it is still not a lush forest. Layers of grasses, shrubs and trees compete for light and nutrients. The impervious rock and level topography trap water in many areas, creating wetland and bog habitats. The naturally acidic conditions encourage the buildup of organic matter (peat) and retain water. Nutrients remain scarce, limiting growth. In a wide clearing, the shortcut road encountered in the Badlands rejoins the route. The open area is a stark contrast to the dense forest. Wildflowers add a splash of color to the dull greens and reds dominating the local coloration. The trail then continues its monotonous route south, with glimpses of the towers by Lake Maratanza providing an occasional beacon.

After a little over a mile, the route encounters the side trail to Indian Rock. From here the route follows the descriptions given in the Indian Rock hike. At the junction with the paved road, two options are available, the shorter route being to the west (right). Both choices provide some excellent views and easy walking.

Along with the hike around Lake Awosting in Minnewaska, High Point is the longest destination the Gunks have to offer. The views, waterfalls and forest habitats along the way are among the range's best scenery. Encompassing the area's highest terrain, the visit to High Point is a definite Shawangunk highlight.

# Sam's Point/Indian Rock Loop

**Hike: Sam's Point/Indian Rock Loop**
**Distance:** 5.00 miles
**Parking:** Sam's Point parking area is east of Cragsmoor at the end of Sam's Point Road. There are a few options for getting into the area, all using NY 52.
**Fees:** Cars $5.00. Yearly pass available.
**Difficulty:** Moderate
**Elevation change:** (lowest to highest points on route): 280 feet
**GPS reference points:**

| | |
|---|---|
| Parking area: | 41°40.211' N, 74°21.654' W |
| Indian Rock: | 41°41.656' N, 74°21.347' W |

**Details:**
0.00 From parking area veer left on paved road.
1.05 Lake Maratanza.
1.20 Junction with High Point Carriageway. Turn left (northeast).
1.50 Junction with yellow-marked Indian Rock Trail.
2.10 Indian Rock.
2.70 Return to High Point Carriageway.
3.00 Rejoin paved road. Turn right (east).
3.30 Pass dam and outlet of lake.
3.85 Pass dirt road leading to Verkeerder Kill Falls Trail.
4.30 Sam's Point.
5.00 Return to parking area. End of hike.

Indian Rock balances above the Shawangunks' western face. Surrounded by a harsh landscape and a simple community of pitch pine, mountain laurel and blueberries, the bold white rock harbors a great view and a bit of legend. Along the route is one of the best views the Gunks have to offer. Like most hikes in the Shawangunks, the trail is not steep, and old carriageways underlie much of the route. To reach

Indian Rock, the route uses an abandoned byway. The hike's most challenging features are the distance and the optional activity of scaling Indian Rock itself.

From the parking area where The Nature Conservancy maintains a small visitor center, the trail begins by bearing left (west) on the paved road. The first part of the hike is a pleasant walk through second-growth forests. The road parallels the stalwart cliffs upholding Sam's Point, a constant looming mass upholding this promontory's western flank. Following a moderate slope, the hard, broken surface makes a pleasant warm-up exercise. Free of tree cover, the road allows more sunlight to reach the ground than in the surrounding forest. Along with increased temperatures on sunny days, the extra sunlight encourages a variety of wildflowers and grasses to thrive along the roadside. A second-growth forest dominated by mountain laurel, chestnut and northern red oak, white ash and red maple covers the slopes. In contrast with the recovering forest, a set of shanty shacks, the summer homes of the huckleberry pickers, interrupts the landscape. The cottages were used by these migrant berry pickers each summer when the occupants would head up the mountain to make some sure money harvesting berries. Although the cottages are in disrepair, even in their heyday these ugly, Spartan structures would never have received much praise for being comfortable or inviting.

The road continues at a moderate grade as it falls in below the strong walls upholding Sam's Point. Roadside ditches hold small pools and support tangles of grasses. On the road's western side a tall forest of oaks, birch and an occasional beech shade the ground while the shrub-covered eastern side rises to meet exposed conglomerate cliffs. Throughout the growing season, bird calls fill the air. Catbirds, blue jays and juncos are common sights and sounds. An abandoned gravel pit, a barren scar, sits along the trail's eastern side. Its stripped slopes bake in the sunlight. Dragonflies zip through the scene, taking advantage of the warmth and nearby water.

More humble shacks and the discarded items associated with them litter the landscape. Decaying roofing shingles cover rotting, collapsing walls that hold rusting stove pipes. Used mainly during the berry-

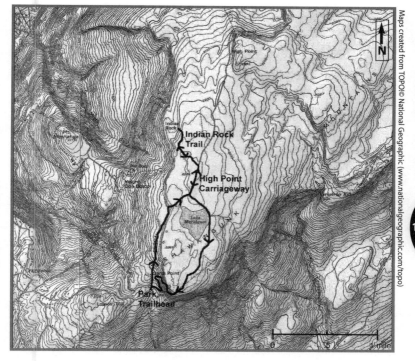

picking season, these small cabins were like working retreats. Old couches, stoves, and other wooden and metal implements make for a rusty monument to past uses of these slopes.

An altered forest community was one result of the huckleberry pickers using this area. Along with the plants normally associated with the Gunks, crab apple, sheep laurel and privet bush also grow here. To improve their lot, cabin occupants would also plant wildflowers for decoration. Clusters of sheep sorrel, buttercup and fire pink still add colorful highlights to the area. The yellow green of hay-scented ferns perfumes the air. The biggest impact of the berry pickers on the environment, however, came from the fires they started to regenerate the berry crop.

Commercial berry picking began during the Civil War, but became more viable in 1901 with the completion of the Smiley Road connecting Ellenville and Lake Minnewaska. Berry prices varied. In the 1860s, eight to fifteen cents a quart was the prevailing price. In the 1920s, pickers could earn a few dollars a day. As the berry economy expanded, the need to preserve this source of income increased. Through periodic burning, the plants competing with the fire-adapted berries could be eliminated, thus promoting future berry crops. These acts of economic arson enraged Shawangunk resort owners and state officials, but were almost impossible to stop; the Gunks' natural ecosystems are designed to burn. To make the burning of the mountain slopes even more enticing, most of the temporary labor employed to fight the fires was recruited from the berry pickers, providing them yet another source of income! As the local economy matured and berries from Maine and other areas became less expensive, the Shawangunks berry picking era came to a close.

The berry pickers were a colorful lot. Most of the pickers gathered together in small communities called camps. Drinking was a favorite pastime. Tales of all sorts of mischief and antics, some bordering on the absurd, remain attached to their local culture. Some used berry picking to scratch out a living, while others used it to gain some extra income. In autumn and winter many of these people would hunt for game, especially deer. Some working-class city folk came to the Gunks to pick berries as a working vacation in the mountain air. Middlemen bought the berries from the pickers and transported them to Ellenville, Middletown and even New Jersey for sale to bakeries and produce markets.

A sweeping curve and one short, steep climb brings the roadway level with the rocks capping Sam's Point and upholding the triangular plateau holding the Gunks' highest elevations. Erosion has eaten into the road, breaking the pavement into chunks of unnatural rock and gravel. Alongside the road, the forest canopy drops and becomes dominated by gray birch, their trunks standing like a regimen of white-uniformed pickets. Scattered conglomerate outcrops produce a more open forest. Pitch pine, the Gunks' signature tree, make their first major appearance in what will become a constant presence on the route to Indian Rock.

Another curve brings the road to Lake Maratanza and the communication towers lining the plateau's western edge. To the east, the lake's clear, almost lifeless waters lap against the unyielding stone. Pitch pines grow wherever their roots can grab a hold among the rocks and shallow, acidic soils. The conglomerate rock wall bounding the lakeshore continues south to Sam's Point. The high ground just south of the lake rises to 2,289 feet, one of the Gunks' twin highest points. To the west a squat tower interferes with a view of the distant Catskills.

The entire area is acid-dominated, but this is unrelated to acid rain. The Gunks' do not have enough fertility in the form of calcium, magnesium and potassium to balance the rainfall's natural acidity, much less the deposition of additional sulfur and nitrogen. One result of the acidic environment is a dead lake. Another is the inability for deciduous trees to survive. When nutrients are plentiful, deciduous trees are better at utilizing them, but in infertile conditions, conifers are more efficient at getting the most from limited resources.

The rocks bordering the lake provide a good view to the west. The towers, a set of landmarks visible from most of the Gunks' higher outlooks, severely detract from the area's wilderness character. On the other hand, they provide a constant navigation and reference beacon, helping orient anyone moving through the area. Through the metal and wire framework, pieces of Slide, Peekamoose, Table and Denman mountains along with Red, Blue and Thunder hills, are visible. Farther south, the lower hills of the southern Catskills cross the Delaware River, where they change identity to become the Poconos. Near the Poconos' southeast corner, the Delaware River breaks through the Appalachian Mountains at Delaware Water Gap. The gap itself is part of the same ridge upholding the Shawangunks.

The paved road works its way around the lake, coming to an intersection with the High Point Carriageway near the lake's northwestern corner. A trail sign notes the left turn (north) to Indian Rock. Surrounded by scrubby trees, metal towers and power lines, the landscape is by no means pristine or attractive, except, perhaps, to the mourning doves roosting on the wires. Still, this community, along with the scruffy, dwarfed vegetation, is unique. Quaking aspen, a fast-growing pioneer species, makes an appearance. Its leaves have flattened stems, so they flex more easily along one axis, resulting in leaves that shake and quake in almost any breeze.

High Point Carriageway is nothing more than a wide dirt road cutting though the Gunks' highest elevations. Both the carriageway and the paved road were improved by the Civilian Conservation Corps in the 1930s. Spur roads and trails, mostly dead ends used by the huckleberry pickers, head off in each direction. Some lead to the radio towers. None are interesting. On a more attractive note, the Catskills' additional 1,900 feet of elevation rising only a few miles away and sitting on the horizon, give the area a more mountainous look and feel.

After about a half-mile, the carriageway has gained about fifty feet and is alongside the Gunks' other 2,289-foot elevation co-champion. Pitch pine still dominates the forest, but the white-trunked gray birch add splashes of brightness to the forest. The area is so flat and the rock so impervious to water that much of the terrain is acidic wetland with many bog-like characteristics. Spongy sphagnum mosses colonize the wet, acidic waters. If enough organic matter accumulates, the area may develop a thick peat layer.

The yellow-marked trail to Indian Rock branches westward from this small rise, just past the innocuous high point. The trail heads into a thick bank of pitch pine, mountain laurel and blueberry. Boggy wetlands on raised platforms line the route. Although this natural community may not be economically valuable or aesthetically attractive, it is essential to the local ecology, as it allows more species to survive and sustains one of the Appalachian's rarest forest communities.

Once off the wooden walkways, the trail becomes an orange-brown line among the yellow-green forest. The encroaching plants shape the trail into a thin, green-walled canyon barely wide enough for one person to pass. The colors and textures are visually stunning, as well as physically imposing. From early July until September, this area is awash in blueberries and huckleberries. The sweet, tasty berries are ample compensation for the cramped quarters.

The trail gradually works its way down slope as it averages a course a little west of north. The trail ground is soft and comfortable, the spent needles cushioning each step. As the land drops, occasional white outcrops of conglomerate interrupt the thick needle carpet with increasing frequency. Dwarfed pitch pine make an appearance on the exposed rocks, their roots struggling to provide support and find water.

Indian Rock is about .6 miles from the carriageway, but another exposed boulder offers a superior view about two-thirds of the way there. The view is among the best in the Shawangunks and rivals any in the state. This five-star view includes parts of Pennsylvania and New Jersey along with an extensive look at the Catskills. In the fore- ground the steep drop of the Gunks' western slopes adds additional layers to the vista. To the north is the isolated, white rock of Indian Rock. Across the Rondout Valley, the Catskills' individual peaks rise like a city skyline. Slide Mountain is the scene's Empire State Building, surrounded by a host of other layered peaks including High Point, Mombaccus, Little Rocky, Peekamoose, Table, Graham, Doubletop, Big

Looking west from above Indian Rock toward the central Catskills

Indian, Lone and Rocky mountains. The large grassy wall holding back the Rondout Reservoir is visible. Another layer of smaller peaks, the same ones visible from the rocks lining Lake Maratanza also are visible. Adding to the delights of the viewpoint is a set of highbush blueberries that provide some of the sweetest berries in the Gunks.

The trail continues to work downhill and to the north providing a good look into the twisted, chaotic pitch pine forest. Slope increases as the path moves off the high plateau. Steeper slopes wash away more of the eroded sediments, creating a rockier and root-studded trail. Open areas begin to work into the dense forest. Glacially scoured and polished rocks become more apparent. Glimpses back to the main Shawangunk ridge appear. Orange and black butterflies, mainly Dianas, toss and tumble in the air.

As the trail nears Indian Rock, it turns and twists among the increasingly complex landscape. Rock cairns help provide guidance, but keen observation skills are needed as well. There is no danger of getting lost, but it can be frustrating when hemmed in by sharp pitch pine needles. With one last twist and descent, the trail emerges at Indian Rock.

It takes a bit of imagination to see Indian Rock as the head of an Indian, but a rough similarity can be made out. This broken slab of Shawangunk conglomerate was moved and shaped by glaciers to give it a softened appearance. Luck placed the rock in its vertiginous, but stable position. A view almost as impressive as the one described earlier is available to those climbing the steep rock icon. This view adds Ellenville, and a feeling of isolation on the exposed perch, but it does not compensate for the smaller perspective.

The boulders below Indian Rock are an example of a rock city, one of the Shawangunks' trademark geologic formations. When the deep-buried rocks now forming the Gunks were softened and deformed into a series of gentle swells and dips during the formation of the Appalachian Mountains, they were slightly stretched at the top of the swells. When exposed to air, water and the other agents of erosion, this stretched rock tends to break and form vertical joints. Ice pushes the joints farther apart, separating the rock masses and forming huge rock "buildings." The buildings at the exposed edge of the cities can tumble onto their sides. This is the process occurring at many of the Shawangunks' cliffs, including those at Indian Rock. The process also forms the ice caves dotting the area; the deep creases remain cold enough to maintain year-round ice.

The return trip to the parking area is enhanced by completing the trip around Lake Maratanza and heading past Sam's Point. The route is a mile longer, but the loop and easy terrain make it worthwhile. To complete this loop around the lake, turn east (left) when reaching the junction with the paved road. After only a short distance the road moves alongside the lake, providing open views across the water.

A cool breeze often moves across the lake—pleasant in summer, bone-chilling in winter. The gauche lake is not picturesque. Located at the top of the Gunks, there are no higher crests to add any mountain charm. Past dredging projects have dumped piles of silt and gravel along the shore. Retaining walls and large awkward rocks square off the lake. The water's color is typically a reflected brown, not the charming shades of blue and green found in the Gunks' other sky lakes. Although not teeming with life, the lake often hosts visiting mallard and black ducks, and other waterfowl. Unwelcome algae thrive in the stagnant areas, fed by the nitrogen and other inputs from atmospheric deposition.

The road crosses the lake's outlet, a small stream joining Verkeerder Kill as it heads over the Gunks' eastern wall. Collapsed pavement marks the outlet's path. The Verkeerder Falls Trail crosses this stream just before the water makes its steep plunge into the Wallkill Valley. One last look at the lake comes from a small cove at its southern edge. The cove has a more flattering viewpoint of the communication towers. Here, grasses and reeds grow in the sandy soil, thriving until the lake levels fall. One reason wetlands are so important is that they act as a natural filter preventing particles and pollutants from entering open water.

After the cove the road remains level, moving through a mixed forest. A few wildflowers, notably asters, heal-all, daisies and blue star grass, dot the roadside. The next major intersection is the junction with the Verkeerder Falls Trail. From here the road heads to Sam's Point and then down to the parking area. This part of the route is described in the High Point-Verkeerder Falls section.

Indian Rock is not a difficult hike. It is a long enough hike to stretch the legs and get away from civilization, but it does not require more than a half-day to complete. The extraordinary view alone makes Indian Rock a destination well-worth the trip. Add in the contrast of nature and man, the views along Lake Maratanza and fresh ripe berries, and this hike can easily become a Shawangunk favorite.

# OFF THE RIDGE

The back side of the Catskill's escarpment from Red Hill,
including High Point and Little Rocky mountains

# RED HILL

**Hike: Red Hill**
**Distance:** 2.2 miles
**Parking:** Off Dinch Road, a dirt road, about 1.2 miles from its
junction with Red Hill Road. Access to Red Hill Road is
from Claryville, located a few miles north of NY55 along
Sullivan County Route 19. Take the county road to Red Hill
Road and make a right. From Red Hill Road make a sharp
left on Dinch Road. The parking area is on the left (west)
side of the road.
**Fees:** None
**Difficulty:** Moderate
**Elevation change:** (lowest to highest points on route): 890
feet
**GPS reference points:**
    Parking area:    41°55.879' N, 74°30.448' W
    Fire Tower:    41°55.428' N, 74°31.042' W
**Details:**
0.00 Follow yellow-marked trail to summit.
1.10 Fire tower. Return via same route.
2.20 Return to parking area. End of hike.

Red Hill is not a part of the Shawangunks, but it offers an extensive overview of the entire range, scanning the ridge for more than fifty
miles. Such a vista would be impossible to gather from the Gunks
themselves. In addition, Red Hill's historic fire tower scanned the eastern horizon spotting many of the fires impacting the Shawangunks
throughout the early and mid-1900s. Part of the Catskill Mountains,
Red Hill stands out along the range's southeastern edge, but its rounded peak can be lost among the higher summits to the north and northwest. The hike up Red Hill is a great opportunity to place the
Shawangunks among their neighboring ranges and get a unique

overview of them, without actually visiting. A walk through Red Hill's northern hardwood forest also adds perspective on how much drier the Shawangunks are than the Catskills.

Nestled north and a little west of the Rondout Reservoir, Red Hill is not easy to reach. The best approaches are from Ellenville and Claryville. Country roads surround Red Hill, but the easiest access is from Red Hill Road, located south of the mountain. A turn north on Dinch Road delivers vehicles along the dirt road to a small parking area. In a slightly cruel gesture, the road passes through a high gap and heads downhill before reaching the trail head. All of this elevation must be regained on foot. The hike is short, only 1.1 miles, but the trail gains 890 feet, making the route challenging even for accomplished hikers.

The road and parking lot easily blend with the recovering forest, but the trail immediately removes even the last hints of traffic and man's major transportation systems. The trail lines the mountainside

Red Hill's fire tower displays the highest peaks of the central Catskills, including Slide, Peekamoose and Table Mountains.

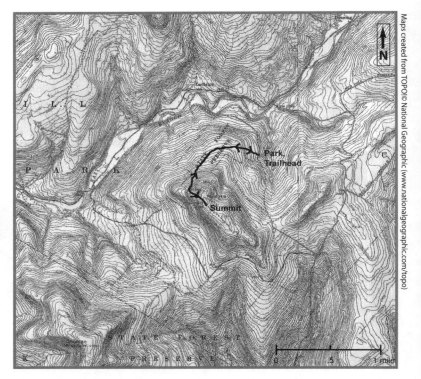

Maps created from TOPO!© National Geographic (www.nationalgeographic.com/topo)

like a soft brown ribbon, a quality it keeps throughout the journey. The trail crosses a few streams soon after leaving the parking lot, but they are often dry in late summer and autumn. Even when parched, the rounded rocks, gravel and mosses fostered by the flowing water attest to the stream's vigor. American beech trees, marked by their smooth, silvery gray bark and yellow-green leaves, dominate the forest. The feathery, dark green needles of hemlock present a striking contrast with the brighter beech leaves.

Beech trees throughout the Shawangunks and neighboring areas face a serious threat. The entire species is under attack from beech bark disease (see page 118). In time the nectria fungus either works its way around the trunk cutting the crown from the roots, or the opening begins to rot and the tree collapses. Either way the tree dies. Subsequent generations of beech grow up with the disease and these black, charred-looking specimens rot and fall well before the tree reaches maturity.

Bird life abounds on Red Hill. One sign of this rich avian community are horizontal lines of small holes found on some of the larger trees, especially hemlock. These are the work of yellow-bellied sapsuckers, members of the woodpecker family. Mostly yellow, white and black, the males sport a distinct red throat patch. Sapsuckers feed mainly on the inner bark and sap of their favorite trees by drilling the lines of horizontal holes in tree trunks and inserting their long, brushy tongue. Insects caught in the sap are another favorite food and an important source of protein. Other woodpeckers and hummingbirds will often visit the holes to steal a sip or two of sap.

With a summit of only 2,900 feet, Red Hill does not offer enough elevation to bring about a major shift in forest composition. The forest floor is often covered by woodland mountain fern and club moss, providing a variety of textures above the crispy, brown leaves carpeting the forest floor. Sugar maple, yellow birch, northern red oak and the species encountered earlier grow all the way to the summit. In a few spots Norway spruce have been planted. Their dark, stiff foliage is easy to distinguish from hemlock's flat, lacy needles.

Throughout the hike the trail alternates between moderate slopes and level areas. This stair-step approach is a direct result of the Catskills' rock strata. Unlike the Shawangunks, whose rock beds lie beneath the Catskills, the Catskills' rock layers run horizontally. Rounded by glaciers and veneered with till, the blocky layers are often buried, but in places the bedrock pokes through the till and soil to reveal its true character. The trail up Red Hill often used the level platforms created by the rock layers to provide a more moderate grade. Along many of the inclines, gray bedrock accompanies the trail uphill. The level areas often drain poorly, and in spring can be very wet and spongy. Striped maple, a flexible understory tree often reaching thirty-five feet, is common beneath the canopy. The large leaves look like a goose foot. Unlike red maple and sugar maple, striped maple leaves turn a pale gold in fall, the tree unable to produce any red pigments. The tree is a favorite food of deer and porcupines. Black cherry, a species with a dark bark that looks a lot like burnt potato chips, does well where gaps open in the forest canopy.

The forests on Red Hill are not very old. The largest trees are only about a foot in diameter, and few have reached their full size. The land was farmed, logged and used as pasture until about seventy years ago. In one area, the trail enters an old meadow. Yellow birch dominate the forest, and the widely spaced smaller trees give the forest a more open feel. Along with a healthy growth of grasses, a host of ferns share the ground. Few dead leaves loiter in the green areas. Hemlocks ring the area, the unused ground beneath them a shadowy contrast with cheery greens. Pileated woodpeckers and black-capped chickadees are common sights.

The trail steepens again after the meadow. Moving through a young forest, again dominated by beech and striped maple, the trail quickly gains elevation. Fallen beech trees open many gaps in the

The level profile of the Shawangunk Ridge is apparent
from the Red Hill fire tower.

canopy, providing an opportunity for black cherry saplings to thrive. Sunlight easily filters through the depleted canopy. The slanted slopes and thin tree cover also provide glimpses of some of the central and western Catskills' highest peaks: Doubletop, Slide, Table and Peekamoose mountains.

The tree height decreases as the trail levels out near the summit. Although the forest composition has not changed much since the parking area, the more exposed slopes have a harsher winter climate, subjecting the forest to ice and wind. As a result tree growth is stunted, bringing the forest canopy closer to the ground. Still, Red Hill is not a high mountain for the Catskills. The trail makes a left turn before emerging into an open field. A sturdy, inviting dark brown cabin greets the hiker. Beyond the cabin rises the steel fire tower. Recently restored, the man-made perch rises well above the thick tree cover.

Sugar maple, beech, northern red oak and Norway spruce dominate Red Hill's summit, making the sixty-foot fire tower the only option for obtaining a view. The climb up the nine flights of steel and wood stairs lifts the viewer above the leaf cover. Views in all directions unfold. Once above the trees, the wind picks up as well, the air no longer contained by the natural windbreak. To the west and southwest rise the Catskills of Sullivan County, including Denman Mountain, Blue Hill and Thunder Hill. Thunder Hill's distinctive open summit makes it an easy-to-recognize beacon from much of the Shawangunks. Along the western horizon the Moosic Mountains outside of Scranton, Pennsylvania, lift above the gentle horizon.

To the north rise the more massive, dominating forms of the Catskills' higher elevations. Millbrook Ridge, Balsam Lake, Graham, Doubletop, Big Indian and Slide mountains form the northern and northwestern horizon. Even closer, looming behind Van Wyck Mountain, are Table and Peekamoose mountains, by far the dominant features from Red Hill. Farther east rise Ashokan High Point, Mombaccus, Little Rocky, and Samson mountains.

From the northeast to the south runs the Shawangunks' long, low ridge. The range is visible from Bonticou Crag south to beyond Sam's Point, where the eye can follow the ridge into New Jersey. Sky Top and the towers along Lake Maratanza are all easily visible. Between Red Hill and the Great Valley lie the sparkling waters of the Rondout Reservoir, another major landmark visible from much of the Shawangunks.

As one of the few remaining and restored towers in the Catskills, the fire tower has a story of its own to share. The tower was built around 1920 as part of the effort to fight fires in the Catskills and Shawangunks. Components were brought up the mountain by horse and buggy. In 1991, it was the last tower abandoned as aerial surveillance became the standard method for spotting fires. It was reopened in the summer of 2000. Restoring the tower required removing, fabricating and replacing some of the steel support braces. Through volunteer efforts, the steel work was completed in nearby Newburgh, New York. The new braces were delivered by helicopter.

Red Hill provides an opportunity to get an overview of the Shawangunks and their relationship to the younger, higher Catskills, which are a major part of the Shawangunks' west-facing views. The hike is also a great opportunity to experience a part of history common to the Catskills and Gunks: watching for fire. While fire monitoring duties now fall to air and satellite surveillance, the chance to get above the trees and share a bird's eye view of both ranges makes the trip a journey full of new perspectives.

# SHAWANGUNK GRASSLANDS NATIONAL
## WILDLIFE REFUGE

**Hike: Shawangunk Grasslands National Wildlife Refuge**

**Distance:** Varies depending on route. One circuit of runways and taxiways is about 3.35 miles.

**Parking:** Off Ulster County Route 18 (Hogerburgh Road), 5.2 miles south of Route 44/55 (via County Route 7) and 4.1 miles north of NY 52.

**Fees:** None

**Difficulty:** Easy

**Elevation change:** (lowest to highest points on route): 20 feet

**GPS reference points:**

Parking area:    41°38.203' N, 74°13.136' W

**Details:**

0.00  Head east into refuge from parking area.

0.40  Reach runways.

1.20  Far end of southern runway.

1.90  Return to runway cross junction. Head left (north) on west runway.

2.45  Far end of western runway.

2.95  Return to entrance road. Turn right (west) to return to parking area.

3.35  Parking area. End of hike.

One of the more curious sights from the eastern side of the Shawangunk ridge is the large airfield in the Wallkill Valley. Twin runways form a lopsided cross and are paralleled by a series of thinner taxiways. On closer inspection, the airfield is overly quiet. There are no buildings in sight and no airplanes either—no takeoffs, no landings. No lights brighten the night. The place is abandoned, a ghost of an airport. When the Galeville Army Airport was no longer needed for our nation's defense, the facility was handed over to West Point Military Academy, but being obsolete, the airfield was not of much use to the military college. The field was used occasionally for special operations training, driver training and parachute drops. In 1999 about 3,500 acres of grassland habitat, including the underutilized airfield, were transferred to the U.S. Fish and Wildlife Service, and became the Shawangunk Grassland National Wildlife Refuge.

Like people, migratory birds use the Shawangunks' long, uninter-rupted ridge as a major landmark. Millions of migrating birds follow the Shawangunk ridge as they head from wintering grounds to breed-ing habitats and back again during spring and fall migrations. Throughout most of the Gunks' route through New York, its ridgeline is paralleled by the Wallkill River and its wide, fertile valley. Many birds stop in the wetlands, forests and fields to rest and eat.

The Wallkill Valley was reshaped by the Wisconsin ice sheet. As the ice moved south, it plowed into the soft rocks and gouged the val-ley floor. Huge quantities of meltwater flowed down the Wallkill Valley seeking a route to the sea when the continental ice sheet retreated 10,000 years ago. Often blocked by ridges to the south and dammed by ice to the north, a number of temporary lakes formed. Whereas the advancing ice sheet widened and deepened the valleys, glacial deposits and rock flours deposited on lake floors filled them in. The result is low, gently rolling terrain with fertile soils.

The excess water from the retreating glacier is long gone, but the fertile wetlands and rich wildlife habitats created by it persist. Farmers have been growing corn, wheat, vegetables and fruits in the area for the past 300 years. Horse farms are also common. More recently, with encroaching development from New York City's growing suburbs, the amount of open land is on the decline. With development so promi-nent, the areas available for migratory birds and other wildlife have been reduced. For these species to find food and shelter, there must be enough habitat for them to use. The refuge is one effort to preserve and enhance grasslands habitats for migratory birds.

The refuge is a place for people as well as wildlife, and it presents some unique wildlife watching opportunities. Although hiking the

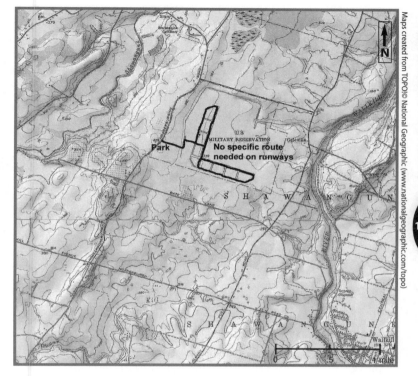

Maps created from TOPO!© National Geographic (www.nationalgeographic.com/topo)

refuge does not compare in difficulty with other hikes in the Shawangunks, the refuge's paths and abandoned runways provide a chance to walk through some great scenery and see a variety of wildlife, especially birds. With two runways, each more than a half-mile long, and an additional quarter-mile walk into the refuge, a basic tour through the refuge becomes a 2.5-mile hike.

Refuge attractions include a sweeping view of the Shawangunk ridge to the north and west, and a chance to observe the more than 150 species of birds known to use this area. Although birds use the refuge year-round, in a typical day during the spring and fall migration seasons, more than seventy species of birds can be seen. Birds range from

Looking toward the Gunks from the refuge

American goldfinches and tree swallows, to short-eared owls and red-tailed hawks. They use the grasslands, forests and wetlands. Some soar, while others bounce up and down in flight to confuse predators.

Since the terrain does not require the exertion or attention needed on the Gunks' trails and carriageways, the easy hiking leaves more time to experience the wildlife and habitats that make this national wildlife refuge a special place. Another benefit to hiking on the refuge is its year-round accessibility. Milder conditions in the Wallkill Valley mean there is less snow and ice to deal with, and the flat ground is more forgiving than icy mountain slopes. Even in winter a host of species use the refuge, including deer, rabbits, squirrels, northern harriers, red-tailed hawks, wild turkey, doves, woodpeckers, tufted titmice, white-breasted nuthatches and black-capped chickadees.

On entering the refuge, located on the east side of Ulster County Route 18, a thin trail, once part of a wider road, passes though aging woodlands and high grasslands. Small forest stands escort the trail to the refuge's more open interior. The deep woods are dark, keeping temperatures down and moisture level up. Woodland ferns grow well in these conditions. As the trail heads east it breaks free of the restrictive tree cover. The land opens, thickly covered by a heavy blanket of grasses. Depending on the season, among the grasses grow a variety of wildflowers, including clover, asters and violets. A variety of lone trees—mainly red maple, northern red oak, dogwood and white pine—also peppers the grasslands.

Among the most entertaining birds to watch is the tufted titmouse. This small gray bird grows up to six inches in length. Sprightly and acrobatic, titmice will hang in almost any position and dart from one tree to another. They hang upside down as they search for food. They eat a variety of invertebrates, such as caterpillars, beetles, wasps, ants, bees, treehoppers, spiders and snails. Titmice get food from tree bark and twigs, but they also forage on the ground. In winter titmice cache seeds and acorns throughout their territories and frequently visit bird feeders. They often forage in mixed flocks with chickadees and nuthatches.

The tufted titmouse is a year-round resident of deciduous and mixed deciduous-coniferous forests in the eastern United States. Titmice prefer habitat with a variety of tree species and a fairly dense canopy. They are adaptable in choosing their nesting sites; practically any opening will do. They will nest in or near swamps, orchards or parks. Both sexes build the nest, typically made of grass, feathers and moss. The females lay six to nine eggs, and are quick to defend their nests.

Although the grasses are a haven for ticks and other insects, they also provide food and shelter for many more desirable species, especially migratory birds. The edge habitat—the area where grasslands transition into forest—are a great place to look for mammals and birds. Deer are common, thriving among the plentiful food and shelter. Unfortunately, the deer are a major vector for spreading ticks. The valley's milder climate allows more ticks to survive the winter than in the nearby mountains. Lyme disease rates in the area are among the nation's highest.

Remaining level and an easy walk, the trail then moves through a wetland area, another prime habitat for birds. A few hundred acres of wetlands are scattered about the refuge, and are the home to some rare plant species, including purple milkweed, small white aster and Frank's sedge, a plant thought extirpated in the state until its rediscovery here in 1992. Red wing blackbirds, nature's spring herald, thrive among the reeds and grasses. Their enthusiastic calls bring the area alive with sound and activity. American goldfinches also zip through the reeds and cattails, their blazing yellow a beacon among the more mundane surroundings. The wetland is also home to frogs, salamanders and turtles. In spring the turtles often migrate through the area as they look for mates and places to lay their eggs. Insects, both pest and benevolent, use the wetland areas to breed and live. Many become food for animals higher on the food chain.

North of the wetland, the Shawangunks' eastern ridgeline lifts from the horizon, the tower on Sky Top a distant, but bold landmark. Throughout the trails and old runways, most of the Gunks' ridgeline is visible. Stretching from just north of Sky Top to the communication towers beside Lake Maratanza, the ridge is a constant companion for the refuge. Many of the hikes that follow the Gunks' eastern edge, such as Gertrude's Nose, Hamilton Point and Verkeerder Falls, offer a look to the south or east that often reveals the runways' huge, lopsided white cross.

The connection between mountain range and refuge is more complex than proximity alone. The Shawangunks' ridgeline protects the refuge from some of winter's harshest fury and provides a major rest area for migrating birds. The mountains provide additional water to the area by creating a small amount of orographic precipitation and delivering water from the mountains into the valley. In addition, the twenty-two-degree tilt of the Shawangunks' topography forms a giant ramp for rising thermals. This natural lift makes the area highly desirable for migrating birds.

The trail then works its way to the open runways of the old Galeville Army Airport. This facility mainly serviced transport planes and served as an emergency landing site. After being removed from the military roles, the property became available for other uses, and the U.S. Fish and Wildlife Service received the property. Through habitat management the large open grasslands are increasing in their value to grassland birds. This refuge, part of a system of refuges and preserved land along the Wallkill River, will help maintain a healthy ecosystem. By conserving and protecting sites all along North America's major flyways within the United States, the National Wildlife Refuge System is an important component of the effort to maintain healthy, functioning ecosystems in the United States.

The runways make for a surreal experience. Equivalent to a seven-lane superhighway, the concrete walkways are outlined by vegetation on all sides. Looking down more than a half-mile of runway in two directions presents bold lines that contrast greatly with nature's random growth. The vegetation, however, is not satisfied to remain along the runways' edges. In the concrete's cracks and joints, hearty grasses and herbs are colonizing the hard ground. Roots reach through the cracks and dig into the tiny soil pockets accumulating among the joints. The vegetation further cracks the concrete, increasing its impact on the ground. Ant colonies become established within the cracks, and insects live on the plants. The insects attract spiders, birds and frogs. Although it is a long process, nature is already taking off to reclaim this sterile, artificial surface.

Following the runways and paths is easy, and little guidance is needed to complete a successful circuit. While traveling along the runways, the landscape's dynamic nature is revealed in its fields, forests and wildlife. Taxiways provide additional areas to walk. Being able to walk out on a runway, even one with wildflowers growing out of the cracks, appeals to the child in almost everyone. Even though the big military planes no longer land here, looking into the sky and seeing the massive jets coming in to land in New York City is quite a thrill.

In contrast with most hikes in the Gunks, the refuge is a noisy place, surrounded by roads. Traffic noise slips through the trees along the refuge edge. The echoes of farm equipment bounce off the hills and slide across the gentle landscape. Unlike the Shawangunk ridge, this area is prime agricultural land. Natural growing processes, hindered by shallow, infertile and too-fast-draining soils on the ridge, are much more effective here. The higher densities of birds, frogs and other vocal species fill the refuge with sound.

Natural process would return this area to forest, but the refuge is managed to retain the grasslands. In the past as grasslands reverted to forest, new grasslands were created by fire, floods, or clearing. Today, with real estate development, much of the region's grasslands have disappeared underneath a growing sea of houses and mini-malls. Species such as Hensley's sparrow, eastern meadowlark and upland sandpipers are declining in number. Places like the Shawangunk Grasslands National Wildlife Refuge help these species to survive.

Located off the Shawangunk ridge, the refuge is often warmer than the mountains, making it a good destination in early spring and late fall. The refuge is also a great place for sunsets, and the wide runways make it easy to return to the parking area in twilight. Since it is easy to access, it also makes for a good walk when time is short. Despite the lack of elevation and the very easy route, the refuge is a great way to get a wider perspective of the Shawangunks.

## ABOUT THE AUTHOR

Ed Henry grew up in the Catskill Mountains, just outside of Woodstock. He has been exploring and writing about the Appalachian Mountains and surrounding regions for the past twenty years, first as a boy scout, then as a writer and photographer. The Shawangunks' long, rugged ridge has been a familiar part of Ed's life. From the sharp form of Snake Hill all the way south to High Point in New Jersey, Ed has hiked and photographed this unique ridge.

Besides his adventures in the Gunks and the Catskills, Ed has worked as a park ranger in the Shenandoah and Great Smoky Mountains National Parks. He also has worked for the U.S. Forest Service, and currently works for the U.S. Fish and Wildlife Service and the 540-unit National Wildlife Refuge System. One of these refuges, Shawangunk Grasslands NWR, is included in this book.

Ed Henry is the author of two books on the Catskill Mountains, Books One & Two of *Catskill Trails: A Ranger's Guide to the High Peaks* (Black Dome Press), plus numerous magazine articles. He has a master's degree in forest ecology from SUNY's College of Environmental Science and Forestry in Syracuse, New York.

Ed lives with his family in western Massachusetts, but frequently returns to his favorite trails in the Gunks and Catskills.

# ROUTES DESCRIBED

**Hike: Bonticou Crag (p. 31)**

**Distance:** 3.75 miles

**Parking:** Spring Hill Parking Area. Located off County Route 6 on Upper Knolls Road, 1 mile west of the entrance to the Mohonk Mountain House and 3.6 miles east of NY 213 via County Routes 6A and 6 from High Falls.

**Fees:** $5 per person, Mohonk Preserve. Yearly membership available.

**Difficulty:** Easy, with a short, difficult rock scramble.

**Elevation change:** (lowest to highest points on route): 550 feet

**GPS reference points:**

| Parking Area: | 41°47.710' N, 74°07.685' W |
|---|---|
| Bonticou Crag: | 41°47.311' N, 74°07.076' W |

**Details:**

0.00 Spring Farm Parking Area—follow dirt road or blue-marked Table Rocks Trail left (east).

0.20 Junction with red-marked Crag Trail. Head right (southeast).

0.40 Cross two carriageways (Cedar Drive and Spring Farm).

0.75 Crag Trail ends at Bonticou Carriageway. Turn left (northeast).

1.05 Junction with yellow-marked Crag Ascent Trail. Turn left (southeast).

1.20 Summit, Bonticou Crag 1,194 feet. Trail heads to left (northeast).

1.50 Crag Ascent Trail ends at blue-marked Northeast Trail. Continue straight (northeast).

2.15 Northeast Crags.

2.30 Northeast Trail ends at red-marked Clearwater Carriageway. Veer left (northwest).

2.75 Join with blue-marked Table Rocks Trail. Turn left (southwest).

3.75 Table Rocks Trail return to parking area. End of hike.

**Hike: Eagle Cliff (p. 42)**

**Distance:** 1.9-mile loop

**Parking:** Take County Route 6 from the east or west side of the ridge. Turn into the Mohonk Mountain House entrance way. Parking areas are located near the entrance and at the hotel. A shuttle is available from the entrance parking area to the hotel.

**Fees:** $15 for car and driver plus $5 additional per individual

**Difficulty:** Easy, with a few steep, rocky spots

**Elevation Change:** (Lowest to highest points on route) 360 feet

**GPS Reference Points:**

| | |
|---|---|
| Hotel: | 41°46.097' N, 74°09.330' W |
| Eagle Ascent Path: | 41°45.696' N, 74°09.694' W |
| Copes Lookout: | 41°45.895' N, 74°09.686' W |

**Details:**

0.00 Start from south end of Mohonk Mountain House at beginning of Eagle Cliff Carriageway. There are also many side trails paralleling the carriageway.

0.50 Reach summit of Eagle Cliff, elevation 1,434 feet. Turn left on red-marked Eagle Ascent Path.

0.60 End of Eagle Ascent Path; turn right (west) on Short Woodland Drive.

0.65 Short Woodland Drive ends at Humpty Dumpty Carriageway. Turn right (north) on Humpty Dumpty Carriageway.

0.75 Turn left on the blue-marked spur trail, which runs into the Giant's Path.

1.05 Giant's Path heads left at the red-marked Arching Rocks Path. Continue straight. For the side trip to Giant's Workshop, turn left and follow the Giant's Path, then return to the Arching Rocks Path.

1.40 Arching Rocks Path ends at the blue-marked Cathedral Path. Turn right (uphill).

1.50 Cathedral Path ends at Copes Lookout. Turn left on Laurel Ledge Carriageway. After only a few steps, the Copes Lookout Path forks to the right.

1.80 Copes Lookout Path ends on Eagle Cliff Carriageway. Turn left.

1.90 Return to Mohonk Mountain House. End of hike.

**Hike: The Trapps and Sky Top (p. 55)**

**Distance:** 7.75 miles

**Parking:** Mohonk Preserve Visitor Center off Route 44/55, .4 miles west of the intersection with the western end of NY 299, and 5.0 miles east of the entrance to Minnewaska State Park Preserve. Other parking is available closer to the trailhead, but time restrictions may apply. Trail begins at Trapps Bridge, which crosses the road 1.1 miles west of the visitor center.

**Fees:** $5 per person, Mohonk Preserve. Yearly membership available.

**Difficulty:** Difficult

**Elevation change:** (lowest to highest points on route): 640 feet

**GPS reference points:**

| | |
|---|---|
| Trail head (Trapps Bridge): | 41°45.804' N, 74°09.347' W |
| Rhododendron Bridge: | 41°45.493' N, 74°09.911' W |
| Smiley Tower on Sky Top: | 41°44.210' N, 74°11.066' W |

**Details:**

0.00 Trail begins at Trapps Bridge. Cross bridge to Overcliff Carriageway (no markings). Turn left (north). Overcliff Carriageway heads generally northeast.

2.40 Overcliff Carriageway ends at Rhododendron Bridge. Cross bridge and turn left (north) on Oakwood Drive.

2.55 Oakwood Drive ends at Old Minnewaska Carriageway. Turn right (south).

3.45 Turn right (east) on Forest Drive.

3.50 Turn left (north) at Mohonk Spring. Trail heads onto open rocky slope and can be confusing. Head for the large crevice in the cliff face and look for the red-marked trail.

3.55 Climb the crevice (one-way up).

3.60 At the top turn left (follow the signs).

3.85 Sky Top Tower, 1,542 feet. On leaving follow the Sky Top Path downhill (northeast).

4.05 Reach staircase to the Labyrinth. Turn left.

4.10 Turn left on Spring Path (can also follow the Labyrinth).

4.35 Return to Forest Drive at Mohonk Spring. Turn right on Forest Drive, then left on Old Minnewaska Carriageway. Trace route back to Rhododendron Bridge.

5.40 Cross Rhododendron Bridge. Turn right (south) on Undercliff Carriageway.

7.75 Return to Trapps Bridge. End of hike.

🚶🚶

**Hike: Millbrook Mountain (p. 70)**

**Distance:** 5.65 miles

**Parking:** Mohonk Preserve Visitor Center off Route 44/55, .4 miles west of the intersection with the western end of NY 299, and 5.0 miles east of the entrance to Minnewaska State Park Preserve. Other parking is available closer to the trailhead, but time restrictions may apply. Trail begins at Trapps Bridge, which crosses the road 1.1 miles west of the visitor center.

**Fees:** $5 per person, Mohonk Preserve. Yearly membership available.

**Difficulty:** Difficult

**Elevation change:** (lowest to highest points on route): 600 feet

**GPS reference points:**

Trail head (Trapps Bridge):     41°45.804' N, 74°09.347' W

Millbrook Mountain (junction with Millbrook Mountain Trail):

41°45.493' N, 74°09.911' W

**Details:**

0.00 Start at Trapps Bridge on Trapps Carriageway and turn left (southwest).

0.05 Turn left (southeast) on the Millbrook Ridge Trail.

0.75 Pass Bayards Path.

1.95 Pass Millbrook Cross Trail.

2.75 Reach eastern crest of Millbrook Mountain, 1,605 feet. Look for red-marked Millbrook Mountain Trail and take a right onto it (northwest).

2.95 Turn right (northeast) on to Coxing Trail.

4.60 Coxing Trail ends at Trapps Carriageway. Turn right (northeast).

5.65 Return to Trapps Bridge. End of hike.

**Hike: Three Falls and High Peters Kill (p. 84)**

**Distance:** 3.40 miles

**Parking:** Lower lot of Minnewaska State Park Preserve, located along Route 44/55, 5.4 miles west of the intersection with the western end of NY 299 and 5.9 miles east of the intersection of route US 209 and Route 44/55.

**Fees:** $5 per car at Minnewaska State Park Preserve. Yearly pass available.

**Difficulty:** Moderate, with one difficult off-trail stretch

**Elevation change:** (lowest to highest points on route): 380 feet

**GPS reference points:**

Parking area:          41°44.102' N, 74°14.673' W

Lowest point (Peters Kill foot bridge):

41°44.673' N, 74°13.198' W

**Details:**

0.00 Start by following road east from parking area. Pass entrance kiosk, cross the Peters Kill, then make an immediate left (east) onto the carriageway paralleling the stream.

0.45 Awosting Falls.

0.85 Carriageway veers left. Leave the carriageway and cross Route 44/55.

0.90 Carefully work down the slope of the north side of the road to reach Sheldon Falls.

1.05 Pass ruins of power plant. Follow the stream down slope until reaching red-marked trail above Peters Kill Falls. Take the trail's left (lower) branch.

1.25 Peters Kill Falls. Continue on red-marked trail.

1.85 Red-marked trail ends at blue-marked High Peters Kill Trail. Turn left (west), cross the bridge and climb the ridge.

2.05 End of steep incline.

3.35 Trail rejoins Route 44/55 just west of the parking area. Turn right.

3.40 Parking area. End of hike.

**Hike: Lake Minnewaska and Beacon Hill (p. 92)**

**Distance:** 3.00 miles

**Parking:** Upper lot of Minnewaska State Park Preserve, located along Route 44/55, 5.4 miles west of the intersection with the western end of NY 299 and 5.9 miles east of the intersection of route US 209 and Route 44/55.

**Fees:** $5 per car at Minnewaska State Park Preserve. Yearly pass available.

**Difficulty:** Easy

**Elevation change:** (lowest to highest points on route): 260 feet

**GPS reference points:**

| | |
|---|---|
| Parking area: | 41°43.102' N, 74°14.699' W |
| Beacon Hill: | 41°44.108' N, 74°13.616' W |

**Details:**

0.00 Begin from upper parking area. Take red-marked Lake Shore Drive Carriageway to the right (west). Keep the lake to the left.

0.95 Cross dam at lower end of Lake Minnewaska. After dam can leave trail and follow shore line or follow Lake Shore Drive.

1.15 Informal shore trail rejoins Lake Shore Drive. Continue uphill to Cliff House site.

1.30 Cliff House site. Cut across open area to lower set of picnic tables.

1.40 Yellow-marked Beacon Hill trail leaves from northeast corner of picnic area.

2.25 Beacon Hill 1,520 feet. Leave via orange-marked Beacon Hill Carriageway.

2.80 Carriageway ends at park's main road. Turn left and follow the road uphill to return to parking area.

3.00 Upper parking area. End of hike.

**Hike: Gertrude's Nose (p. 103)**

**Distance:** 6.70 miles

**Parking:** Upper lot of Minnewaska State Park Preserve, located along Route 44/55, 5.4 miles west of the intersection with the western end of NY 299 and 5.9 miles east of the intersection of route US 209 and Route 44/55.

**Fees:** $5 per car at Minnewaska State Park Preserve. Yearly pass available.

**Difficulty:** Moderate

**Elevation change:** (lowest to highest points on route): 550 feet

**GPS reference points:**

Parking area:               41°43.102' N, 74°14.699' W
Gertrude's Nose:         41°41.676' N, 74°14.910' W
Millbrook Mountain Trail junction:
                                      41°45.493' N, 74°09.911' W

**Details:**

0.00 Begin from upper parking area and take red-marked Lake Shore Drive Carriageway to the right (west).

0.80 Take right (southeast) on yellow-marked Millbrook Drive.

1.05 Veer left, remain on Millbrook Drive.

2.00 Leave carriageway and continue straight on red-marked Gertrude's Nose Trail.

2.50 Cross power line.

3.00 Gertrude's Nose.

3.80 Cross power line.

4.70 Reach junction with red-marked Millbrook Mountain Trail. Turn left (north).

5.10 Cross Coxing Kill.

5.85 Return to southern end of Lake Minnewaska and Lake Shore Drive. Turn right. (east), but can go around lake either way.

6.15 Cliff House site.

6.70 Upper parking area. End of hike.

**Hike: Hamilton Point and Castle Point (p. 114)**

**Distance:** 7.60 miles

**Parking:** Upper lot of Minnewaska State Park Preserve, located along Route 44/55, 5.4 miles west of the intersection with the western end of NY 299 and 5.9 miles east of the intersection of route US 209 and Route 44/55.

**Fees:** $5 per car at Minnewaska State Park Preserve. Yearly pass available.

**Difficulty:** Moderate-Difficult

**Elevation change:** (lowest to highest points on route): 580 feet

**GPS reference points:**

| | |
|---|---|
| Parking area: | 41°43.102' N, 74°14.699' W |
| Hamilton Point: | 41°41.992' N, 74°16.255' W |
| Castle Point: | 41°42.205' N, 74°16.433' W |

**Details:**

0.00 Begin from upper parking area and take red-marked Lake Shore Drive Carriageway to the right (west).

0.80 Take right (southeast) on yellow-marked Millbrook Drive.

1.05 Veer right onto yellow-marked Hamilton Point Carriageway.

2.25 Cross power line.

3.40 Hamilton Point.

3.70 Turn right (northwest) on Long Path.

3.80 Castle Point. Continue on Long Path (to the left)

5.15 Junction with green-marked Awosting Carriageway. Turn right (east).

7.50 Reach northwest corner of Lake Minnewaska. Turn left (east) on Lake Shore Drive.

7.60 Upper parking area. End of hike.

**Hike: Lake Awosting (p. 128)**

**Distance:** 9.95 miles

**Parking:** Lower lot of Minnewaska State Park Preserve, located along Route 44/55, 5.4 miles west of the intersection with the western end of NY 299 and 5.9 miles east of the intersection of route US 209 and Route 44/55.

**Fees:** $5 per car at Minnewaska State Park Preserve. Yearly pass available.

**Difficulty:** Difficult

**Elevation change:** (lowest to highest points on route): 560 feet

**GPS reference points:**

Parking area:                        41°42.102' N, 74°14.673' W

Eastern (lower) end of Lake Awosting:

                                     41°42.697' N, 74°16.926' W

**Details:**

0.00 Leave the parking area via the black-marked Peters Kill Carriageway. Almost immediately, turn left (southeast) on yellow-marked Mossy Glen Trail.

1.65 Mossy Glen Trail ends at blue-marked Blueberry Run Trail. Turn left (south).

1.85 Junction with green-marked Awosting Carriageway. Turn right (west).

2.10 Cross power line.

3.30 Awosting Carriageway ends at black-marked Awosting Lake Shore Road. Turn right (west). Begin loop around the lake.

4.90 Reach far end of lake.

6.60 Complete loop, continue along bottom of lake (small amount of overlap).

6.70 Peters Kill Carriageway heads right (north) from the Awosting Lake Shore Road.

7.15 After crossing Fly Brook, make left on blue-marked Jenny Lane Trail (also Long Path).

7.60 Cross power line.

8.20 Junction with blue-marked Blueberry Run Trail. Turn right (south).

8.40 Junction with Peters Kill Carriageway. Turn left (northeast).

9.95 Return to parking area. End of hike.

**Hike: Stony Kill Falls (p. 139)**

**Distance:** 1.20 miles

**Parking:** End of Shaft 2A Road, off Rock Haven Road. Rock Haven Road is just off Route 44/55, 1.5 miles east of the intersection of Route 44/55 and US 209. If coming from the east, it is a right turn (not well marked) and then an immediate left. From the west, it is two left turns. Take Rock Haven Road 1.9 miles, then turn left on Shaft 2A Road.

**Fees:** None at parking area. The falls are in Minnewaska State Park Preserve, which charges a fee.

**Difficulty:** Easy

**Elevation change:** (lowest to highest points on route): 75 feet

**GPS reference points:**

Parking area: 41°43.814' N, 74°17.897' W

Eastern (lower) end of Lake Awosting:

41°43.669' N, 74°18.075' W

**Details:**

0.00 From parking area follow the stream or informal trail (generally south and west) up the gentle grade.

0.30 Pass through cleared area.

0.60 Stony Kill Falls. Return using the same route.

1.20 Return to parking area. End of hike.

**Hike: Verkeerder Kill Falls and High Point (p.147)**

**Distance:** 8.90 miles

**Parking:** Sam's Point parking area is east of Cragsmoor at the end of Sam's Point Road. There are a few options for getting into the area, all using NY 52.

**Fees:** Cars $5.00. Yearly pass available.

**Difficulty**: Difficult

**Elevation change:** (lowest to highest points on route): 500 feet

**GPS reference points:**

| | |
|---|---|
| Parking area: | 41°40.211' N, 74°21.654' W |
| Verkeerder Falls: | 41°41.115' N, 74°19.671' W |
| High Point: | 41°42.229' N, 74°20.671' W |

**Details:**

0.00 Take left fork of paved road on leaving parking area.

0.65 Sam's Point.

1.25 Leave paved road. Turn right (southeast) on dirt road.

1.30 Turn left (east) on blue-marked Verkeerder Kill Falls Trail.

3.05 Verkeerder Kill Falls.

3.25 Turn left (north) on red-marked High Point Trail (can be hard to follow at times).

5.65 High Point, elevation 2,246 feet.

6.00 Old fire tower site. Head left (downhill) to High Point Carriageway.

6.10 High Point Carriageway. Turn left (southwest).

7.75 Rejoin paved loop road encircling Lake Maratanza. Turn right (west).

8.90 Return to parking area. End of hike.

**Hike: Sam's Point/Indian Rock Loop (p. 159)**

**Distance:** 5.00 miles

**Parking:** Sam's Point parking area is east of Cragsmoor at the end of Sam's Point Road. There are a few options for getting into the area, all using NY 52.

**Fees:** Cars $5.00. Yearly pass available.

**Difficulty:** Moderate

**Elevation change:** (lowest to highest points on route): 280 feet

**GPS reference points:**

| Parking area: | 41°40.211' N, 74°21.654' W |
| Indian Rock: | 41°41.656' N, 74°21.347' W |

**Details:**

0.00 From parking area veer left on paved road.

1.05 Lake Maratanza.

1.20 Junction with High Point Carriageway. Turn left (northeast).

1.50 Junction with yellow-marked Indian Rock Trail.

2.10 Indian Rock.

2.70 Return to High Point Carriageway.

3.00 Rejoin paved road. Turn right (east).

3.30 Pass dam and outlet of lake.

3.85 Pass dirt road leading to Verkeerder Kill Falls Trail.

4.30 Sam's Point.

5.00 Return to parking area. End of hike.

**Hike: Red Hill (p. 170)**

**Distance:** 2.2 miles

**Parking:** Off Dinch Road, a dirt road, about 1.2 miles from its junction with Red Hill Road. Access to Red Hill Road is from Claryville, located a few miles north of NY55 along Sullivan County Route 19. Take the county road to Red Hill Road and make a right. From Red Hill Road make a sharp left on Dinch Road. The parking area is on the left (west) side of the road.

**Fees:** None

**Difficulty:** Moderate

**Elevation change:** (lowest to highest points on route): 890 feet

**GPS reference points:**

| | |
|---|---|
| Parking area: | 41°55.879' N, 74°30.448' W |
| Fire Tower: | 41°55.428' N, 74°31.042' W |

**Details:**

0.00 Follow yellow-marked trail to summit.

1.10 Fire tower. Return via same route.

2.20 Return to parking area. End of hike.

**Hike: Shawangunk Grasslands National Wildlife Refuge (p. 177)**

**Distance:** Varies depending on route. One circuit of runways and
taxiways is about 3.35 miles.

**Parking:** Off Ulster County Route 18 (Hogerburgh Road), 5.2 miles
south of Route 44/55 (via County Route 7) and 4.1 miles north of
NY 52.

**Fees:** None

**Difficulty:** Easy

**Elevation change:** (lowest to highest points on route): 20 feet

**GPS reference points:**

Parking area:     41°38.203' N, 74°13.136' W

**Details:**

0.00 Head east into refuge from parking area.

0.40 Reach runways.

1.20 Far end of southern runway.

1.90 Return to runway cross junction. Head left (north) on west
runway.

2.45 Far end of western runway.

2.95 Return to entrance road. Turn right (west) to return to parking area.

3.35 Parking area. End of hike.